MINDFULNESS: TO LEARN THAT ALL LIVES CAN'T MATTER UNTIL BLACK LIVES MATTER

THAT WE ALL DESCEND FROM THE SAME
MATERNAL WOMB

JAIME CARLO-CASELLAS, PH.D.

Mindfulness: To Learn That All Lives Can't Matter Until Black Lives Matter
— That We All Descend from the Same Maternal Womb

ISBN: 978-1-7337980-1-3

Robert Teitelbaum Publishing

Other books by the author:

Mindfulness for the Common Man: To Survive Trauma, Abuse, and Recovery

Anguish & Joy / Amargura y Deleite: A Journey to Serenity / Una jornada hacia la felicidad

Chaos & Bliss / A Journey to Happiness: Poetry and Verse to Enlighten the Mind / Caos y Éxtasis: Una jornada a la Felicidad: Poemario para iluminar la mente

Chaos & Bliss: A Journey to Happiness: Poetry and Verse to Enlighten the Mind — Second Edition/ Caos y Éxtasis: Una jornada a la Felicidad: Poemario para iluminar la mente — Segunda Edición — In Press

Cover image by Evelyn Artaud-Carlo, with permission. Cover design by Jaime R. Carlo-Casellas, Ph.D.

Introduction

I was wondering what my good friend and mentor Jaime Carlo-Casellas was up to when he asked if he could include one of my blog posts I call Communiqués. The subject was how the US Confederacy validated slavery as part and parcel of the "natural", you know part of God's master plan, to support white supremacy as the only reason necessary to continue practicing the enslavement and degradation of human being peripherally different from one another. I was intrigued to say the least. Where was Dr. Jaime going to go with this? How was a history lesson in cruelty going to translate to mindfulness? When I got my draft, I found out. And it was revelatory.

When I saw the words "Black Lives Matter" my first thought was "Huh?" What in the world did Dr. J have up his sleeve? Then I began to read. At first, I remember thinking "he's not trying to tie together mindfulness, chemistry/physiology, and improving one's social conscience for a better life for all, is he? Is he suggesting by looking within, changing ourselves if necessary, by elimination of the hateful illusion we call racism, society, meaning all of us would be better off for it? By changing our anger and angst into curiosity and respect regarding God given trails and co-incidentally something we have no actual control over (race/creed/color) into a loving perspective of non-judgmental learning and acceptance? I continued reading, hoping. . .

Well, as of this writing, I don't know if that was JCC's actual intent. But that's what I got, in spades and I couldn't have been more delighted with his combination of the physical, meta-physical, and get this the practical applications of mindfulness to eliminate the scourge of prejudice that still plagues us individually, and as a nation. When will we all accept the simple fact that we were all born of the same maternal womb? Additionally, how?

We begin by changing ourselves. By realizing we have formed over the years the bad "habit" of learned, negative assumptions about our brothers and sisters who we don't know anything about, thereby passing to opportunity to listen with an open heart and an open mind to the struggles, victories and yes, wisdom that they may or may not be able to share, simply because they are in many instances ethnically different than "us"?

As with all true change, it begins within. Mindfulness does not judge. It does not care if you are a practitioner of intolerance or the one being subject to intolerance. It only gives you the opportunity to "see" what is often, if not always, right before your eyes, if only you are willing to acknowledge there must be another way, a better, brighter, and more holistic way of being. Of nurturing your mind, body, and soul, and in doing so, enhancing the lives of all others while we have this time together on Earth.

For you the reader, this is my question for you. You have in your hands the practical tools of mindfulness techniques. For those of you who are more science than faith oriented, you have the chemical and electro motor functions to explain why mindfulness on the physical level will produce tangible, physical change. And now, for the first time I have ever seen such a connection, to support the Black Lives Matter movement to promote social and economic justice and in the process, tear down the walls of ignorance that prevent us all from sharing in the unlimited bounty of being and enjoying the fruits of another person's simply left to the best that we can all be.

So simple really, for after all, I don't know about you, but who would I be to not strive to be the best I can be and then extend this greatest of gifts to all my brothers and sisters that, as I said earlier, are all from the same maternal womb. Any other actions seem illogical, irrational, and possibly a failure of morality.

When you embrace that we are all one, you will know you cannot help yourself by hurting those who you were born to exhibit love, kindness and caring towards. You can only hurt yourself. I humbly suggest you don't do that, especially now that you have your marching orders. Black Lives Matter. If you are already there, congratulations. If not, it is never too late to do the right thing, starting right here and right now. Flip the page and be wise. I dare you.

Philip Drucker

College of the Desert
California Desert Trial Academy College of Law

"Look at other people and ask yourself if you are really seeing them or just your thoughts about them . . . Without knowing it, we are coloring everything, putting our spin on it all."

~ Jon Kabat-Zinn

To those who believe in our homogeneity…
that we all descend from the same maternal womb.
A todos los que creen en nuestra homogeneidad…
que todos descendemos del mismo vientre materno.

THANK YOU

"As we express our gratitude, we must never forget that the highest appreciation is not to utter words, but to live by them."

~ John Fitzgerald Kennedy

I am forever indebted to Jon Kabat-Zinn, Ph.D. and Saki Santorelli, Ed.D., my first meditation teachers, who in the mid-1980s guided me through the eight-week Mindfulness-Based Stress Reduction Program (MBSR) at the University of Massachusetts Medical School. It was Jon and Saki who led me to recognize my purpose in life. From them I learned that you only die once, so I learned to recognize that life is the most extraordinary and prodigious event into which I have been invited.

My appreciation goes to Zindel Segal, Ph.D., for my training in Mindfulness-Based Cognitive Therapy to decrease the risk of the depressive relapses I used to encounter and to Alan Marlatt, Ph.D., for the training he provided in Mindfulness-Based Relapse Prevention.

I would like to thank Robert W. Hollenbeck for his devotion, love, insight, and helping me by copyediting this book.

I am grateful to María del Socorro Guzmán Muñoz, Ph.D., from the Department of Humanities and Social Sciences at the University of Guadalajara, Mexico, who edited the Spanish version of my first book, *Chaos & Bliss,* and who wrote the introduction to and edited my second book, *Anguish & Joy.* Because of the impact Socorro has on her students and her understanding of those in need, the world is a much better place in which to live. When I reflect on my interactions with Socorro, I am reminded of the words of Father Lawrence G. Lovasik: "By being kind, we have the power of making the world a happier place in which to live, or at least we greatly diminish the amount of unhappiness in it so as to make it a quite different world."

To my friend and mentor, Father Benedict Reid, I extend my reverence for instilling in me the notion that the perfect doctrine is the one you design yourself, most pointedly the one that propels you to explore and fill the empty well within you.

Interest in writing this work is due in great part to my friendship with Philip Drucker, one of the deans and Professor of Constitutional Law at the California Desert Trial Academy College of Law, who was kind enough to write the introduction to *Mindfulness for the Common* Man and this book. Dean Drucker is a firm believer in the concept that all people deserve the right to fully exercise their autonomy, that as autonomous persons they should be capable of self-legislation and able to make judgments and actions based on their particular set of values, preferences, and beliefs.

But most of all I bow to those who took to the streets all over the United States and across the planet to scream forcefully that *Black Lives Matter* after the murder of George Floyd on May 25, 2020. It was this, the most significant civil rights movement in the history of mankind, that sparked interest in writing this book.

PROLOGUE

"Time and again, racist ideas have not been cooked up from the boiling pot of ignorance and hate. Time and again, powerful and brilliant men and women have produced racist ideas in order to justify the racist policies of their era, in order to redirect the blame for their era's racial disparities away from those policies and onto Black people."

~ Ibram X. Kendi

This book is dedicated to those who have come to the Stress Management & Prevention Center, LLC, seeking relief from disparagement, stigmatization, and denigration by society at large — Hispanics, those from the LGBTQ community, those seeking racial justice, those suffering from mental disorders, and particularly those who bear the pain and concern of "All Lives Can't Matter Until Black Lives Matter."

Together we ultimately conclude that *we all descend from the same maternal womb.*

Before proceeding, it is important to note that much of what appears here, by necessity, comes from my previous work, *Mindfulness for the Common Man: To Survive Trauma, Abuse, and Recovery.*

The Heritage Foundation is shining a light on America's biggest issues so that we can begin to work together on solutions. The Foundation's mission is "to formulate and promote conservative public policies based on the principles of free enterprise, limited government, individual freedom, traditional American values, and a strong national defense."[1]

Notwithstanding its mission, until the notion of white supremacy is abrogated from the fabric of our being, racism against people of color and Hispanics, homo-aversion, misogyny, bigotry, and the suppression of human rights will continue to be common practice in our society.

Then it happened!

> MINNEAPOLIS, June 1, 2020[2]: Both the Hennepin County Medical Examiner's office and an autopsy commissioned by George Floyd's family have ruled that the death of Floyd — in an incident that has triggered nationwide unrest — was a homicide and the forty-six-year-old's heart stopped beating while police restrained him and compressed his neck.
> The medical examiner's report released Monday listed

"cardiopulmonary arrest complicating law enforcement subdual, restraint, and neck compression" as the cause of death. It came hours after Floyd family attorney Benjamin Crump held a press conference to announce the findings of a family-commissioned autopsy. The family autopsy stated "asphyxiation from sustained pressure was the cause" of Floyd's death. Dr. Michael Baden and Dr. Allecia Wilson performed the autopsy and said there was "neck and back compression that led to a lack of blood flow to the brain," Crump said Monday.

They added that "weight on the back, handcuffs, and positioning were contributory factors because they impaired the ability of Mr. Floyd's diaphragm to function."

Floyd died May 25 after a Minneapolis police officer knelt on his neck for several minutes while he was hand-cuffed on the ground, crying that he couldn't breathe and pleading for help. The incident has galvanized outrage, sparking protests and violence throughout the US. Monday's medical examiner's report indicates that its finding "is not a legal determination of culpability or intent and should not be used to usurp the judicial process."

That autopsy found "no physical findings that support a diagnosis of traumatic asphyxia or strangulation," according to the document, which suggests Floyd's existing health conditions — coronary artery disease and hypertensive heart disease — combined with being restrained by police and any "potential intoxicants in his system" contributed to his death.

Baden and Wilson said it appeared that Floyd died at the scene.

We live in a society that for centuries has been challenged by the bromide and delusion that "All Men are Created Equal." Since its foundation, our country has been tested by three juggernauts — slavery, usurpation of territories, and puritanism, or if you will, imposition of unwelcome, often pernicious, dogmas, all of which have led to the belief in white supremacy.

Intelligence

Let us consider skin color and intelligence. To start with, all modern humans share a black-skinned common ancestor who lived around 200,000 years ago in Africa.[3] To quote from the Oxford biologist John R. Baker's book, *Race*,[4] one of the most comprehensive works written on the subject: "There is no evidence that any gene concerned in the control of skin color has any effect on the mental capacity of human beings."

Homo erectus were the first of the hominins to emigrate from Africa, and, from 1.3 to 1.8 million years ago, this species spread through Africa, Asia, and Europe. One population of *Homo erectus*, also sometimes classified as a separate species, *Homo ergaster*, remained in Africa and evolved into *Homo sapiens*.[5]

Neither race nor ethnicity define intelligence. Those who have attempted to measure intelligence among different people, especially people of color and Hispanics, have done so primarily using Intelligence Quotient (IQ) tests. IQ tests have been used for decades to assess intelligence, but they are fundamentally flawed because they do not consider the complex nature of the human intellect and its different components, and using them alone to measure intelligence is a "fallacy." The results of such tests disprove once and for all the idea that a single measure of intelligence is enough to capture all of the differences and nuances in cognitive ability that we see between people.[6]

Blacks and Hispanics

Colonization and slavery, as carried out by European countries, became a matter of concern with colorism and racism since the beginning of modern history. This led to the belief that people with dark skin were uncivilized, inferior, or the "weaker race," and should be subordinate to lighter-skinned invaders. This belief exists to an extent in modern times as well.[7]

Applying this "weaker race" philosophy to Hispanics, Roosevelt, in 1906, indicated, "It is Manifest Destiny for a nation to own the islands which border its shores . . . [I]f any South American country misbehaves it should be spanked."[8] In fact, President William Howard Taft candidly proclaimed this right later on in 1912: "The whole hemisphere will be ours in fact as, by virtue of our superiority of race, it already is ours morally."[9]

Homophobia

Let us proceed with homophobia, or more correctly, homo-aversion, to describe the antipathy to homosexuality. Some still consider it an evil *choice* and not a force of nature. For instance, some claim that excessive masturbation leads to homosexuality; others that children of gay parents grow up to be derelicts, that homosexuals will convert innocent children into homosexuals, or that homosexuals by nature abuse children sexually.

But let's stop calling it a choice. Biological factors drive homosexuality. According to Benjamin Neale,[10] a geneticist at the Board Institute of the Massachusetts Institute of Technology and Harvard University said, "I hope that science can be used to educate people a little bit more about how natural and normal same-sex behavior is. It is written into our genes and it's part of our environment. This is part of our species and it's part of who we are." Another recent study by Keiser[11] shows that genetics may explain up to 25 percent of same-sex behavior.

Misogyny

Gender inequality in the US has been declining significantly throughout our history, beginning mostly in the early 1900s. Nevertheless, in spite of this progress, gender inequality in the US continues to prevail, including disparity in political representation, occupational segregation, and the unequal distribution of labor. The improvement of gender inequality has been the goal of several major pieces of legislation since 1920 and continues to the present. Still, as of 2018, the World Economic Forum ranks the United States fifty-first in terms of gender equality out of 149 countries.[12]

Strafing the Infodemic of Superiority

One important way of strafing away the infodemic of superiority is through *mindfulness*. That i s, b y t raining t he m ind s o as t o change the structure and function of the brain in positive ways through what is known as "neuroplasticity." Via this modality, our society can squelch the opprobrium of ignoring the words in our Declaration of Independence: "We hold these truths to be self-evident, that *all men are created equal,* that they are endowed by their Creator with certain unalienable Rights, that among these are Life, Liberty and the pursuit of Happiness." (Emphasis mine.)

Neuroplasticity

The term "neuroplasticity" was first used by the Polish neuroscientist Jerzy Konorski in 1948 to describe observed changes in neuronal structure.[13] He also proposed the idea of gnostic neurons. These are any hypothetical neuron in the visual-association cortex that is stimulated only by complex and meaningful stimuli, such as a particular individual (e.g., one's grandmother).[14]

Today we know that "neuroplasticity" is a term used to describe the brain changes that occur in response to experience. There are a variety of mechanisms of neuroplasticity. These range from the growth of new neural connections to the creation of new neurons. We know that during meditation, structural and functional changes take place in the brain, allowing improvements in information processing, memory recall, problem solving, and inculcation of loving kindness.[15]

Mindfulness

The thesis proposed here is that through *mindfulness*, we can become aware of who we are as *Homo sapiens* and begin to acknowledge that we are selfless, or as my philosophy professor friend facetiously used to say, "We are nothing but little blasts of flatulence in a big cesspool of humanity." We must recognize that all of us descend from the same maternal womb and that our purpose in life is to be happy, make others happy, and alleviate the suffering of those who suffer. Anything else we do in life is for naught or at least nothing more than trying to reach heightened levels of well-being.

So, what is *mindfulness*? The person credited with introducing mindfulness to Western medicine is Jon Kabat-Zinn, Ph.D.,[16] who in 1979 founded the Mindfulness-Based Stress Reduction (MBSR) program at the University of Massachusetts School of Medicine to treat the chronically ill.

The program uses a combination of mindfulness meditation, body awareness, and yoga to help people become more mindful. The program has been found to be beneficial in reducing the pernicious effects of stress, inducing relaxation, and improving the quality of life, but it does not help prevent or cure physical disease. While MBSR has its roots in spiritual teachings, the program itself is secular. Since then, the application of mindfulness in medicine for the treatment of a variety of conditions in both healthy and unhealthy people has expanded at a worldwide level.

Kabat-Zinn defines mindfulness as:

"...the awareness that arises from paying attention, on purpose, in the present moment and non-judgmentally."

With all that being said, despite all of the discrimination that has been going on in our country since it was founded, no lives will matter until black lives matter.

1

MINDFULNESS IN THE WESTERN WORLD

"To think in terms of either pessimism or optimism oversimplifies the truth. The problem is to see reality as it is."

~ Thích Nhất Hạnh

Our human experience is without meaning or unworthy of analysis until we *mindfully* recognize what it means to be happy, until we question why we habitually inflict unhappiness on others, where the seedbed of loathing and odium resides.

As you will find in this book, it is now well-known that mindfulness can help you reap a cauldron of benefits, not to mention reach higher brain functioning, as well recognize that "All Men are Created Equal."

Some think otherwise. So, let us address the issue of morality. For centuries, philosophers have divided their thinking into two camps. Thomas Hobbes and Jean-Jacques Rousseau represent the most famous opposing views. Hobbes believed that humans are nasty and brutish creatures, believing that we are born corrupt and that society and rules continue to corrupt us. Rousseau, on the other hand, argued that we are gentle and unadulterated beings. He condemned society for degrading our innate goodness. Aristotle claimed that morality is something we learn, and that we are born as "amoral" beings. And Sigmund Freud considered that newborns start from a moral blank slate.

So, are we born with this innate goodness or do we cultivate it as we grow?

Scientists also posited that babies were born without any moral standing — until recently. Research by Razzetti, from Yale University, shows that children are born with a sense of morality — they don't start, as many believed, from a blank slate. The study revealed our basic instinct to prefer friendly behaviors over malicious ones. [1]

Regrettably, but with time, demagogues, ecclesiastics, our parents, grandparents, siblings, pedagogues, the government, and society at large catalyze a process that often transforms many us into monsters of hatred toward others — even ourselves, with feelings of superiority or inferiority — into terrorists, into beasts that use excessive or unnecessary force. It grows and gets boosted as we mature.

"Good people do not need laws to tell them to act responsibly, while bad people will find a way around the laws."

~ Plato

Fighting Archetypes

In attempting to survive this catastrophe, we find ourselves struggling to become unreachable archetypes, something that obliquely resonates within ourselves. Many of us instinctively know what we are striving for: to live by the mandates framed by our forefathers in our Constitution and Declaration of Independence — documents that predicate our equality.

Yet if we were asked to define the archetype we are attempting to reach, we would be hard-pressed to come up with a precise definition. Perhaps it would be something like, "That Goliath of energy that transcends time and place . . . the man on the pedestal, who really believes that 'Black Lives Matter.'"

There is absolutely no doubt that we are transient, living expressions of Nature. We are born, we live, and eventually, like it or not, we die. And how I envy those blessed by their reliance on everlasting life, or for that matter, those who are blessed by their reliance on reincarnation!

So, why are we born? The bigger question might be, how come we were born in Borneo, Puerto Rico, Spain, the United States, Mexico, male, female, heterosexual, homosexual, bisexual, transsexual, with black skin, with blue eyes, without arms, wealthy, poor, etcetera? The fact is that we cannot change who we are — we have to accept ourselves.

I passionately believe, as I have said before, that we have been invited to live on this planet to enjoy life, to be happy, make others happy, and alleviate the suffering of those who suffer. It's a commitment we must make to ourselves — to be of service to others. Anything else we do in life is for naught, or at least nothing more than trying to reach for heightened levels of well-being.

Gratitude

We must also consider *gratitude*. As Mirka Knaster[2] tells us: "Gratitude is essential to living this life fully, to living the holy life: gratitude for the caring presence of others, gratitude for the means not only to survive but to thrive and to share our resources with others. Yet, surprisingly, thankfulness is not listed as one of the qualities or factors that lead to awakening. But that doesn't mean it's not part of the Dharma path. Deep gratitude is the wholesome motivation that underlies the manifestation of those qualities."

A simple practice I suggest is that before going to bed at night, you make a list of five things for which you are grateful. And as you are making your mental list, lie back quietly and watch your breath, breathing in through your nose and exhaling slowly through your mouth. Noticing the inflation of your belly or your torso as you inhale and its deflation as you exhale through your mouth.

With that in mind, many of us soon realize that we are not going to be able to gallop through life without being aware of the horse we are riding. We must be aware of the fact that:

"The right time to be happy is now. The right place to be happy is here, wherever you are, and as long as you are breathing, there is more right with you than there is wrong, no matter how ill or how hopeless you may feel."[3]

We all have goals and aspirations. They reflect our desire to be happy. What is crucial to remember is that as we witness the insolence and denigration of the human person by those who feel superior unfold before our very eyes, as sentient human beings it should be indisputable for us to recognize our *raison d'être*.

Modern medicine aims to improve mental health with psychotherapy and pharmacotherapy. However, it is now well documented that mindfulness can help overcome these hindrances to happiness, enabling those affected by stress to live the lives they seek and deserve.[4]

Meditation as a Tool in Western Medicine

"Mindfulness" for the relief of stress has been around for a while, but unlike many other practices, there is substance behind it. Whether you are dealing with the regular stresses of an overly busy life or something more serious such as a mental disorder, you will find that mindfulness will help you improve your sense of selflessness, loving kindness, and respect for others. Your sense of superiority will start to evanesce as you recognize that you are nothing more than one of the little "tilets" (as in the poem "Mosaic") that makes up the mosaic of humanity.[5]

People throughout the world have been practicing meditation for thousands of years. Yet, as stated before, the person credited with introducing "mindfulness" to Western medicine is Jon Kabat-Zinn, Ph.D. in 1979.

Problem

A major problem with the practice of mindfulness is that often those who practice it, and even some clinicians, associate the practice with religious rituals or even voodooism.

This continues to be of concern, notwithstanding the fact that the Oxford English Dictionary[6] defines mindfulness as:

> *"A mental state or attitude in which one focuses one's awareness on the present moment while also being conscious of, and attentive to, this awareness. Also: the cultivation and practice of this, esp. as a therapeutic technique."*

Furthermore, the American Psychological Association[7] defines it as:

> *"...a moment-to-moment awareness of one's experience without judgment. In this sense, mindfulness is a state and not a trait. While it might be promoted by certain practices or activities, such as meditation, it is not equivalent to or synonymous with them."*

Also, when we practice any mindfulness, we abide by the so-called "eight guidelines of mindfulness":

1. **Non-judging**: Not getting caught up in our ideas and opinions, likes and dislikes.

2. **Patience:** An understanding and acceptance that sometimes things must unfold in their own time.
3. **Beginner's Mind:** Seeing things with fresh eyes, with a clear and uncluttered mind.
4. **Trust:** Believing in your intuition and your own authority.
5. **Non-striving:** Trying less and being more.
6. **Acceptance:** Coming to terms with things as they are.
7. **Letting Go:** Letting our experience be what it is.
8. **Compassion:** To yourself and other sentient beings.

Conclusion

We live in a country in which tradition has challenged us with three quixotic dilemmas — slavery, usurpation of territories, and puritanism — yokes and pillories that, with braggadocious force, have led us to believe in the superiority of the Caucasoid.

Again, as Dr. Martin Luther King, Jr. said, "Morality cannot be legislated, but behavior can be regulated. Judicial decrees may not change the heart, but they can restrain the heartless."

And why mindfulness? Recent research provides strong evidence that practicing non-judgmental, present-moment awareness (aka mindfulness) changes the brain, and it does so in ways that anyone working in today's complex world, and certainly every leader would benefit by learning how to practice it.

Mindfulness improves information processing, it sharpens memory recall, it encourages loving kindness, it teaches selflessness, and it shows us how to rescind the belief in the superiority of the Caucasoid. It teaches us that:

"All Lives Can't Matter Until Black Lives Matter."

2

CURRENT ADMINISTRATION ENCOURAGES WHITE SUPREMACY AND RACIAL INJUSTICE

"There is a cult of ignorance in the United States, and there has always been. The strain of anti-intellectualism has been a constant thread winding its way through our political and cultural life, nurtured by the false notion that democracy means that 'my ignorance is just as good as your knowledge.'"

~ Issac Asimov

The presidency of Donald J. Trump began at noon EST on January 20, 2017, when he became the forty-fifth president of the United States, succeeding President Barack Obama.

The following day, when he was inaugurated, the Women's March, along with a worldwide protest in solidarity, was the largest single-day protest in US history.[1] The protest was due to Trump's statements, considered by many as misogynistic.

A Trump administration official later responded to the women, condemning them for the alleged complaints against the president.

A Debacle for Our Nation — The Onset of a Reign of Terror

To quote from Wikipedia:[2]

> "While Trump lost the popular vote by nearly three million votes, he won the Electoral College vote, 304 to 227, in a presidential contest that American intelligence agencies concluded was targeted by a Russian interference campaign. Trump has made many false or misleading statements during his campaign and presidency. The statements have been documented by fact-checkers, with political scientists and historians widely describing the phenomenon as unprecedented in modern American politics. Trump's approval rating has been stable, hovering at high-30 to mid-40 percent throughout his presidency.

> Trump rolled back numerous environmental protections, as well as reduced enforcement of existing regulations. He ended the Clean Power Plan, withdrew from the Paris Agreement on climate change mitigation, and urged for subsidies to increase fossil fuel production, calling man-made climate change a hoax. Trump failed in his efforts to repeal the Affordable Care Act (ACA) but took numerous actions that hindered its functioning

and sought to have the courts rule it unconstitutional. Despite pledges made as a candidate, President Trump sought substantial spending cuts to Medicare, Medicaid, Social Security, and food stamps. He enacted a partial repeal of the Dodd-Frank Act (that had previously imposed stricter constraints on banks in the aftermath of the 2008 financial crisis), hindered the Consumer Financial Protection Bureau in policing fraud and protecting consumers, and withdrew from the Trans-Pacific Partnership. Trump signed the Tax Cuts and Jobs Act of 2017, which lowered corporate and estate taxes permanently, and lowered most individual income tax rates temporarily while increasing them for some. He enacted tariffs on steel and aluminum imports and other goods, triggering retaliatory tariffs from Canada, Mexico, and the European Union, and a trade war with China. These tariffs adversely affected the US economy. For most of Trump's term until 2020, the economy kept improving, following trends from the Obama presidency. The federal deficit soared under Trump due to spending increases and tax cuts."

Psychological Opinions

According to an article in Politico, his own niece, who holds a Ph.D. in clinical psychology from Adelphi University in New York, states that Donald J. Trump lacks the mental disposition to lead our country.[3]

The article goes on to say that "Mary Trump, the daughter of the president's deceased older brother Fred Trump Jr., accuses the president of paying a friend to take the SAT for him when he was applying to college as a teenager."

"Besides believing that her uncle fits the nine DMS-5 criteria of clinical narcissism,[4] Mary Trump, as well as other mental health professionals, believe he also may suffer from antisocial personality disorder, dependent personality disorder, and a 'long undiagnosed learning disability that for decades has interfered with his ability to process information.'"

These professionals have recognized that Trump is mentally ill, which explains much of his unpredictable and erratic behavior, "making him profoundly unsuited to be president." This cadre of professionals includes more than 70,000 mental health professionals who consider Mr. Trump as potentially dangerous, despite the established professional bans against "diagnosing" public figures who have not been personally examined by a licensed therapist.[5]

Yet, Dr. Bandy Lee[6] indicates, "No doubt, the physician's responsibility is first and foremost to the patient, but it extends 'as well as to society.' It is part of professional expectation that the psychiatrist assess the possibility that the patient may harm himself or others. When the patient poses a danger, psychiatrists are not merely allowed but mandated to report, to incapacitate, and to take steps to protect."

Although psychologists personally would like to "arm-chair" analyze Donald Trump, it is easy to see that indirectly they have been doing so fairly regularly for a couple of years now, albeit certainly not in a formal way. Mental health professionals merely need to observe behavior to tell you that an individual is profoundly disturbed. By observing Trump's behavior, psychologists conclude that he is not well. Whether they're right or wrong is not the issue. "But trust us," these healing-arts professionals say, "the exact disorder doesn't matter; the fact is that Trump definitely s uffers from moderate to severe psychopathology. To put it in language that the lay person is sure to understand: The man is nuts![7]

Animosity Toward the Puerto Ricans and the Hispanic

Trump's animosity toward the Puerto Rican and Hispanics in general is clearly reflected i n h is illegal withholding of aid to the Islanders following Hurricane María. Lawmakers had to inter- vene and say that the Department of Housing and Urban Devel- opment (HUD) was breaking the law by missing a congressionally mandated deadline to make $10.2 billion avail- able in hurricane aid to the Island.[8]

As a result of this, the Island suffered significantly.[9]

The scale of Hurricane María's destruction was devastating, causing as much as $94.4 billion in damages — a crippling toll for an island that was already billions of dollars in debt. The hurricane left thousands of families without homes and totally devastated entire communities. In August 2018, the official death toll was estimated to 2,975 people — forty-six times higher than the original count of sixty-four deaths.

Approximately 80 percent of the Island's crops were wiped out completely, representing a $780 million loss in agricultural yields. This was a devastating blow to an island with high poverty and an already-fragile food supply.

Basic infrastructure, like the power grid and water systems, were almost completely devastated. It wasn't until August 2018, nearly a year after the storm, that Puerto Rico was able to restore power to most of its population. It was the largest blackout in US history.

Fortunately, entrepreneur Elon Musk, from Tesla, has followed through on his plan to boost power resources in Puerto Rico after it was devastated by Hurricane María by setting up solar panels and energy storage batteries at Hospital del Niño, a children's hospital in San Juan. The batteries provided energy from the panels when sunlight was scarce.[10]

Interestingly, just a few days ago, to highlight the nature of his antipathy toward the Islanders, on July 12, 2020, CNN reported that in 2017 Trump had considered the idea of selling Puerto Rico after the Island was devastated by Hurricane María.[11]

Children in Cages

Mr. Trump's family-separation policy is an aspect of his corrupt immigration policy that deserves mention. The policy was part of his "zero tolerance" approach intended to discourage illegal Mexican immigrants from entering the United States. It was emplaced along the entire US–Mexico border from April 2018 and lasted until at least October 2019. Subsequently, it was found that such practice had begun a year prior to the public announcement.

Under Trump's policy, Border Patrol agents separated children from their parents or guardians as they entered the United States. The parents were arraigned and incarcerated while the children were placed under the supervision of the US Department of Health and Human Services. In January 2020, the Southern Poverty Law Center (SPLC) stated that the official government number of children separated from their parents or guardians numbered as many as 4,368, although the number is more than likely much higher.[12]

On October 19, 2018, United Nations' independent experts proclaimed that "Separating children from their undocumented parents is a traumatic violation of their rights."[13]

Deaths as a result of these human rights violations are not as uncommon as one might expect at these centers. In one case, a sixteen-year-old Guatemalan young man was diagnosed as having influenza at an overcrowded center where "basic hygiene doesn't exist." Following his medical examination, he was transferred to a shared cell at a different facility. A Border Patrol spokesperson *explained* that guards checked on Vasquez throughout the night (emphasis mine). However, in the morning, Vasquez was found unresponsive and dead.[14]

He is one of several immigrant children who have died in US detention centers since its beginning in 2019. A terrifying pattern began to emerge. As children are taken into custody, especially those who are ill, they are placed indefinitely in detention and deprived of essential amenities such as clean clothes, sanitary napkins for menstruating young teens, showering facilities, toothbrushes, and other basic toiletries.

Canada Responds to the Outcries of the Caged Children

As a result of these human rights violations, a Calgary, Canada immigration agency stated that Canada should expect another wave of migrants and asylum seekers as America's controversial zero-tolerance immigration policy continues to grab headlines around the world. The agent quoted the mayor of Calgary as saying, "Citizens must do their part to help stop the way the United States is treating those crossing its southern border."[15]

Moreover, in an editorial in Canada's *The Star*, many Canadians have responded to the outcries of children who have been separated from their parents at the US-Mexican border.[16]

> "Like so many of my fellow Canadians, I have been horrified by how the United States Department of Homeland Security has separated at least 2,000 children from their families since April 19.
>
> We have seen the dehumanization of these children as they cower in cages facing wall-sized murals of the president's face, bear arms with identification numbers written in lieu of personal names, and have heard their cries while border officials crack jokes about them.
>
> These migrants have risked their lives as they walked toward the US border, seeking refuge from violence and extreme poverty only to have the wealthiest and most powerful country in the world deny them basic human dignity.
>
> It is easy to think we can relax on our summer patios, congratulate ourselves on being compassionate, enlightened

Canadians rather than cruel Americans, but that would ignore both broader truths and opportunities where Canada could make a positive difference for these (and similar) refugees, but has not."

COVID-19 Among Caged Children

To reference from a recent *New York Times* report:[17]

"Concerned that thousands of these migrant children held in federal detention facilities could be in danger of contracting the coronavirus, a federal judge in Los Angeles ordered the government to 'make continuous efforts to release them from custody.'

The order from Judge Dolly M. Gee of the United States District Court came after plaintiffs in a long-running case over the detention of migrant children cited reports that four children being held at a federally licensed shelter in New York had tested positive for the virus.

The threat of irreparable injury to their health and safety is palpable, the plaintiffs' lawyers said in their petition, which called for migrant children across the country to be released to outside sponsors within seven days, unless they represent a flight risk.

There are currently about 3,600 children in shelters around the United States operated under license by the federal Office of Refugee Resettlement, and about 3,300 more at three detention facilities for migrant children held in custody with their parents, operated by the Immigration and Customs Enforcement agency.

Advocates for immigrants have tried for decades to limit the government's ability to detain children apprehended after crossing the border, arguing that it is psychologically harmful, violates their rights, and undermines their long-term health.

Now, some say the coronavirus represents an even more immediate threat.

In addition to the four children who tested positive in New York, at least one child is in quarantine and awaiting results of a test for the virus at a detention facility operated by the Immigration and Customs Enforcement (ICE) agency, according to documents filed with the court.

In her ruling on Saturday, the judge declined to order an immediate release of all the detained children, given current travel restrictions and the need to ensure that children are released to suitable sponsors, most often family members.

She said, however, that both of the agencies operating migrant children detention facilities must, by April 6, provide an accounting of their efforts to release those in custody.

'Her order will undoubtedly speed up releases,' said Peter Schey, co-counsel for the plaintiffs in the court case.

Judge Gee's jurisdiction stems from a 1997 consent decree, known as the Flores agreement, that established a twenty-day limit on the secure detention of migrant children, as well as standards for their care.

In September, Judge Gee rejected new regulations that would have let the government hold children and their parents in detention for indefinite periods, one of the Trump administration's signature efforts to curtail the large number of families that had been arriving from Central America.

In her order, Judge Gee said the plaintiffs had a strong likelihood of succeeding with their claim that both ICE and the refugee resettlement office had breached the Flores agreement by failing to release minors in a prompt manner, especially in light of the widening coronavirus outbreak."

Trump's Policy on COVID-19 Pandemic

The president's response to the COVID-19 pandemic emulates his longstanding casual disregard for science for political purposes. He has repeatedly contradicted medical experts in favor of his own judgment. But a disdain for scientific advice has been a defining characteristic of Mr. Trump's administration.[18]

Another *faux pax* was the fact that Trump couldn't stop fabricating the efficacy of and advocating for the use of hydroxychloroquine as a treatment against COVID-19.

Hydroxychloroquine, used for decades as a medication to treat malaria and lupus, had generated by far the most excitement within the Trump administration, despite a lack of scientific evidence of its effectiveness against COVID-19.

The debate escalated when Trump effectively halted Dr. Anthony Fauci, the nation's leading infectious disease expert, from answering a question about the drug during a White House press briefing. Over that weekend, the press reported that Fauci had been berated by Trump's economic adviser, Peter Navarro, for calling evidence supporting hydroxychloroquine's use as "anecdotal."

As a result of his mismanagement of the pandemic, as of May 18, 2020, the United States leads the world in the number of COVID-19 deaths.

To make matters worse, on June 21, 2020, Trump used his comeback rally to try to define the upcoming election as a choice between national heritage and left-wing radicalism, but his intended show of political force during the pandemic drew thousands short of a full house and was partly overshadowed by new coronavirus cases among his campaign staff. The rally was meant to restart his reelection effort less than five months before the November election.[19]

Three days later, on June 23, 2020, Trump traveled to Arizona, visiting Yuma to see a recently built section of his border wall, and then heading to Phoenix for a campaign rally at a church. The venue, located in a coronavirus hot spot, was reportedly filled to capacity, with no social distancing inside and few attendees wearing masks.[20]

And on the day before the Fourth of July, when many Americans were struggling with the racist misdeeds of our country's heroes and confronting a merciless COVID-19 pandemic, Trump was dividing, rather that uniting, America. With his histrionic, desultory speeches, he used the backdrop of Mount Rushmore in South Dakota to stir fear of cultural change while denouncing the most basic scientific evidence about the pandemic we are facing. Full of reactionary remarks, he claimed that his opponents, with intents of "ending America," were engaged in a "merciless campaign to wipe out our history, defame our heroes, erase our values, and indoctrinate our children."[21]

Another predicament our country is confronting is the opening of schools. Yes, let's open them and let COVID-19 continue to spread like wildfire. We are at the mercy of our Secretary of Education, Betsy DeVos, who was born with a silver spoon in her hand. Her education, most of it private, consists of Holland Christian High School, whose motto is to "Equip minds and nurture hearts to transform the world for Jesus Christ," and a Bachelor of Arts degree in business economics —not pedagogy — from Calvin College, hardly an Ivy League institution. So, what qualifies her to be Secretary of Education and send our children to the ovens?

Racism and Bigotry

"As long as there is unreasoning bigotry instead of understanding and tolerance, our Nation will fall short of its full power and greatness."

- John F. Kennedy

Donald Trump is well-known for his chauvinism and for making racist jokes and humiliating women, gays, and the handicapped.

Perhaps most revealing is when corporate America remains silent against Trump's bigotry. To some people's disdain, many heads of corporations are clandestinely funding the reelection of a president whose political agenda began with a racist conspiracy theory and who continues to encourage white supremacy. This goes beyond mere hypocrisy. America's most wealthy have accumulated more capital and power than at any time since the late nineteenth century.

Even from early on, Donald Trump publicly questioned if President Barack Obama was born in America. He had long fanned the conspiracy theory of "birtherism," spending much of his time garnering attention and constantly claiming, without any evidence, that Obama was not born in America.

Commutation of Felons

Also, Trump is known for his irrational commutation of felons. For example, on July 11, 2020, Robert Muller spoke out on Trump's commutation of Roger Stone. "The jury ultimately convicted Stone of obstruction of a congressional investigation, five counts of making false statements to Congress, a nd tampering with a witness. Because his sentence has been commuted, he will not go to prison. But his conviction stands. The bottom line: "When a subject lies to investigators, it strikes at the core of the government's efforts to find the truth and hold wrongdoers accountable," Mueller writes. "It may ultimately impede those efforts… The women and men who conducted these investigations and prosecutions acted with the highest integrity. Claims to the contrary are false."[22]

Conclusion

Trump represents a fundamental problem in our society. One can only conclude that he is a catastrophe, a man who arouses fear and whose bailiwicks seem to be prevarication, making unfounded claims, adversity, racism, inhumanity, and conceit. He is an obscurantist, a maverick agitator of humanity, our country, and the world at large, a bellwether who believes in the power of the Caucasoid, not recognizing that there is no such thing as "race."

At a time when nothing seems normal, one thing is clear: he provides an incredible lesson on what not to do and what not to be like. A man unfit for the presidency.

One must learn from him . . . let's make America kind again. Unlike him, let's acknowledge that "All Lives Can't Matter Until Black Lives Matter."

3

BLACK LIVES MATTER MOVEMENT

". . . look at other people and ask yourself if you are really seeing them or just your thoughts about them . . . Without knowing it, we are coloring everything, putting our spin on it all."

~ Jon Kabat-Zinn

On May 25, 2020, America and the entire planet was brought to its knees.

A video footage, as well as official documents, reconstructed the death of George Floyd, a forty-six-year-old Black man, after a convenience store employee called 911 and told the police that Mr. Floyd had bought cigarettes with a counterfeit twenty-dollar bill.

Seventeen minutes after the police arrived at the scene, Mr. Floyd was handcuffed and then pinned down by the knee of Derek

Chauvin, a white police officer, for eight minutes and forty-six seconds. Floyd kept saying "I can't breathe" and supplicating for his mother's help. Shortly thereafter, Mr. Floyd was unconscious, showing no signs of life — he had died.

The documentation showed that the officers had taken a series of actions that violated the policies of the Minneapolis Police Department, leaving Mr. Floyd unable to breathe, even as he and onlookers called out for help.

His death triggered the "Black Lives Matter" protests in over 2,000 cities across the United States and in a plethora of cities around the world against police brutality, racism, and lack of police accountability — perhaps the most historic civil rights movements in the world.[1]

The sound of "Black Lives Matter" reverberated throughout our planet.

Although these manifestations occurred amidst one of the world's worst pandemics, apparently the protests, according to research by the National Bureau of Economic Research, using data on protests from more than 300 of the largest US cities, found no evidence that coronavirus cases grew in the weeks following the beginning of the protests, even though these demonstrations caused a decrease in social distancing among actual protesters.[2]

Nonetheless, the incident and the protests make it clear that racism, bigotry, homophobia, misogyny, and discrimination are still alive and doing well in the United States, the land of the free and the home of the brave.

Let's Defund the Police

"Defunding the police" was all the rage in America as a result of the protests.

And I totally understand the anger behind this. Especially after watching the entire eight minutes and forty-six seconds of George Floyd's agonizing, slow-motion homicide under the knee of Derek Chauvin, who'd had eighteen previous complaints of using excessive force.

To reference from *Citizen Times*:[3]

> "Chauvin, along with the other two officers involve in the case, frequently had used racial slurs, including calling Black citizens, 'negro,' 'niggers,' and 'We are just gonna go out and start slaughtering them fucking niggers.'"

In short, our police departments unquestionably need reform, and lots of it, and much better surveillance. And yes, in some cases, we need to start over. Think way outside the box. Dismantle and rebuild.

As a country, we should consider funding more social workers and mental health professionals to work closely with the police. We should spend more on social programs for youth, and we definitely need real civilian surveillance of police departments, which have entrenched civil service protections that make it difficult to get rid of problem officers.

But totally dismantling our police forces, in my opinion, would be out of the question.

Let's Burn Down Atlanta

One of the demands of the protesters was to dismantle all monuments and symbols of the Confederacy.[4]

Why is this so? Removing and challenging the symbols of the Lost Cause[5] is an important step to dismantling white supremacy, but it cannot be the only step.

In the Philip Drucker Communiqué *Racist RF* in the *Los Angeles Times*,[6] he states:

> "Much like the gun nuts today who think their Second Amendment Rights are 'absolute' (they are anything but), an abbreviated take on the rights of white males to own slaves in the Confederate South would similarly read as 'shall not be infringed.' The actual quote is as follows.
>
> 'No… law denying or impairing the right of property in negro slaves shall be passed.'
>
> However, in terms of real and potential impact upon the culture of the Confederacy, there is a stark and quite frankly alarming 'difference of opinion' contained within the Southern Man's supposed 'rights' to own slaves and all rights commensurate with that, as I said above, God-given right. Namely, that all men are not created equal. Simple but effective and terrifying, really.
>
> At the time of the Civil War, this grand twisting of everything natural and holy and is the very basis of the US Constitution was routinely described among Southerners as the 'Great

Truth' and the basis of why they and their cause alone was blessed by God.

Remember how in Dred Scott the SCOTUS punted on the issue of who and/or what constituted a 'person' under the Constitution? And relegated slaves to the status of 'property' thereby denying them any of the protections guaranteed under the Constitution? And, assigning each slave a 3/5th of a person status for purposes of the Census which in reality was a way for plantation owners to receive additional federal funding for the maintenance of their property and enterprise?

Southern Man chucked that Jim Crow two-step right out the door. There is no other way to explain it except inequality among the races as the law of the land. That's right. Inequality and oppression as a way of life. Make no mistake this is the cornerstone of 'culture' the South wants to pass down.

This is why we are still fighting about monuments to losers. This is why we are fighting about flying the Confederate Battle flag in front of government buildings. And yes, this is why we are still fighting about institutionalized lynching as a 'way of life.' All part of a culture worth passing down. Hatred, racism, inequality, violence, and degradation all approved by the Creator as part of the grand scheme and eternal glory.

And who were these supposed defenders of all that is just and right? According to the CSC, only white men were able to vote and best population estimates of the time put that number at roughly 1.5 million persons out of a total of 11 million inhabitants subject to the Confederacy and all its inhumanity as a way of life.

Did I mention the Civil War only lasted four years? Need I remind you those who fought for the South were traitors and yes, last time I looked they lost? So, why are we still fighting these so-called 'culture wars'?

The unfortunate answer is when the 'Lost Cause' is finally eradicated from our daily lives, so will the 'God-given right' to practice institutionalized hatred, racism, and inequality among all persons as a way of a good and just life, or culture, will be gone with the wind.

Do we really have to burn Atlanta to the ground again? I hope not."

Conclusion

The Black Lives Matter Movement brought America and the world to its knees. A clear distinction between superiority and inferiority was brought to light — that for centuries, pigmentation of skin had served to discriminate and victimize the person of color.

Despite the fact that there seems to be a desire for many to feel superior, let me state the reality that there is no such thing as a *superior race*. In fact, a *race* doesn't exist.[7] Anthropologists, geneticists, biologists, and psychologists came to that conclusion decades ago. Race is something that is intrinsic in our biology, and therefore inherited across generations.[8]

Ethnicity, on the other hand, recognizes differences between people, mostly on the basis of language and shared culture — the clothes we wear, the foods we eat, our music and dance, or our prose and poetry.

As I stated previously, neither race nor ethnicity define intelligence. Those who have attempted to measure intelligence among different people, especially people of color and Hispanics, have done so primarily using Intelligence Quotient (IQ) tests, which are fundamentally flawed because they do not consider the complex nature of the human intellect and its different components. Using them alone to measure intelligence is a "fallacy."

For centuries, as a result of such fallacies, many of us have developed and enjoyed deeply ingrained feelings of superiority and privilege.

Only through mindfulness — *the awareness that arises from paying attention, on purpose, in the present moment and non-judgmentally* — will we be able to begin to:

- Remember that we all descend from the same maternal womb. Each and every one of us experiences fear, shame, pride, love, and carry red blood within our veins. Each one of us carries forty-six chromosomes within our cells. All of us are simply trying to make it.
- Learn to recognize and understand our own privilege.
- Examine our own biases and consider where they may have originated.
- Validate the experiences and feelings of people who are different from us.

- Refrain from telling jokes about those who are different from us.
- Invest in a random act of kindness.
- Invest in charities that fight against injustice and violence.
- Find out how our company or school attempts to expand opportunities for those who are different.
- Remember that all forms of oppression are wrong.
- Learn that "All Lives Can't Matter Until Black Lives Matter."

4

BENEFITS OF MINDFULNESS

"Give your attention to the experience of seeing rather than to the object seen and you will find yourself everywhere."

~ Rupert Spira

indfulness offers us a cauldron of benefits — from the reduction of stress to the management of psychological disorders. To enumerate them here, I reference what I have already stated in *Mindfulness for the Common Man*.[1]

Lower the Levels of Indefatigable Stress and Helps You Relax

Mindfulness meditation recruits your body's parasympathetic nervous system, switching you from the *fight-flight-freeze* to the *rest-relax-digest* state. This results in a lowering of the levels of the stress hormones (cortisol, epinephrine, and norepinephrine) and an increase in the levels of the "feel-happy" neuropeptides (serotonin, oxytocin, the ß-endorphins, dopamine, glutamate, melatonin, gamma-aminobutyric acid (GABA), and acetylcholine). Studies have shown that this phenomenon happens even when one is not meditating but has trained the mind to be aware of what is happening in the now.

Not only does mindfulness immediately calm you when practiced, it strengthens your ability to be aware of the impact that emotional and external stimuli have on your mental and physical well-being. It's empowering to know that you can respond, rather than react, to the unpredictability of life.

Being present in the moment can help calm your nerves in the multitasking, over-stimulating world we live in today. It also draws your mind away from pain, anger, sadness, trauma, and worrying.

These are lifelong techniques that, once learned and espoused, can be summoned whenever necessary to reduce the levels of stress.

Improves Sleep

The clients who have come to our center who suffer from insomnia report that when they have problems falling asleep, they use the sympathetic breathing method or the loving kindness intervention they were taught as tools to help them fall asleep.

Lessens or Eradicates Chronic Pain

The power of becoming the unattached observer of our physical sensations, chronic pain, thoughts, and emotions is what helps us lessen the frequency of our negative outlooks and boosts the frequency of the positive ones. This can come into use with the plethora of stress-related disorders.

Several mindfulness interventions have been shown to reduce or eradicate chronic pain. Mindfulness-based interventions help patients separate the cognitive and emotional experience from the sensory components of pain, leading to a changed experience that carries the potential to reduce suffering. At our center we have found that the most effective interventions are the body scan, sympathetic breathing, and autogenics.

Mitigates the Symptoms of Cancer

Although mindfulness cannot take away the symptoms of the disease completely, it can certainly make the distress, anxiety, and fatigue associated with its treatment more manageable.

Linda E. Carlson, Ph.D., has been offering mindfulness-based cancer recovery programs to people with cancer for approximately twenty years due to the ability of mindfulness interventions to ameliorate common concerns including loss of control, uncertainty about the future, distress, depression, anxiety, fear of cancer recurrence, and unpleasant physical symptoms such as fatigue, pain, and sleep disturbance.[2] Cancer-related fatigue (CRF), one of the most common, persistent, and disabling symptoms associated with cancer and its treatment, was found to be significantly reduced when the patient was taught mindfulness-based stress reduction.[3]

Guards Against Mental Illness

In working with clients with mental health issues, we have witnessed that mindfulness is an important intervention in the treatment of many mental conditions and behavioral disorders such as depression, anxiety, addictive behavior, post-traumatic stress, and bipolar disorders. By calmly observing self-defeating thoughts, cravings, and urges in a non-judgmental way, the client can learn to curb the symptoms of these conditions and down-play their adverse effects. Mindfulness has the power to change perspectives and give them the freedom to choose healthier patterns of behavior.

This is what one client had to say after attending several of our mindfulness yoga classes:

> *"Dr. Jaime, I want to thank you for what you have done for me. I have attended many yoga classes in the past, but until I started coming to you, I had never experienced a yoga class such as yours. I've come to realize that the postures and their proper alignment are not as important as I thought they were. Since I have been coming to your mindfulness yoga classes, the improvement in my symptoms of depression and anxiety, as well as my ability to focus on what's available to me in the present moment, have been incredible — not to mention the strength and flexibility I have gained. Even my husband and my children have commented on what a different person I've become. Another important thing I want to mention is that I no longer rely on the antidepressants I had to take."*

It is normal for the brain to get trapped, or wrapped up, in aberrant streams of thought which can obscure the client's sense of reality. Mindfulness can help the client recognize that thoughts are nothing more than a cluster of neurons firing off, resulting in angst or nightmares. It also helps them see that happiness, sadness, pain, and pleasure are ever changing and impermanent. By practicing the mindfulness interventions we offer, clients begin to see that life is constantly changing — a perfect reflection of the absurdity of life.

Contributes to Self-Confidence and Self-Compassion

These are arguably two of the most valuable benefits of developing a mindfulness meditation practice. Without self-confidence and self-compassion, it is hard to achieve the kind of life you want to live. Most physical and psychological ailments make it difficult to feel your best and believe the goals you have set are attainable.

Mindfulness practice is, at its core, a process of self-discovery that can lead to total liberation. The knowledge that you are always your true self and that you are not defined by your thoughts, anxieties, fears, or experiences lets you know that you are in control.

During yoga, when practicing the warrior pose (*Virabhadrasana*), our facilitators often tell the participants, "As you hold this pose, take a moment to think about the *power, confidence, strength,* and *assertiveness* of the warrior within you!"

As one of my client's husband said, "I don't know what you've done with my wife. She's still the same wife, but something is different, she is more sure [sic] of herself, more assertive, and much more affectionate."

Although we are born with innate goodness and without any feelings of right or wrong, inferiority or superiority, quickly many of us have the need to feel superior.

The impulse to continually evaluate our own selves, is costly. To be called *average* is considered offensive.

"Did you learn anything from my lecture last night?" "Not really." Yikes!

Notwithstanding, the great anguish of modern life is that no matter how hard we try, no matter how successful we are, no matter how good a parent, worker, or spouse we are — it never seems to be enough. We always meet someone who is wealthier, thinner, brighter, or stronger than we are. And failure of any kind is unacceptable — narcissism is ingrained in so many of us. So, what to do?

Thousands of books and magazine articles promoting self-esteem have been written about the subject. It has almost become a cliché in our culture that we need to be *perfect* to be happy and healthy.

Yet, it is so easy to achieve self-acceptance. All one has to do is practice *loving kindness* — toward our own selves, our loved ones, our friends, those who are different from us, strangers, those who cause us difficulties, and all sentient living beings on the face of this planet.[4]

Facilitates Healing

Mindfulness cannot only help a patient deal with a chronic or potentially terminal illness, a life-threatening event, or surgery, but it can also help the patient recover from such conditions.

One of the classes we offer is dedicated to patients who are coping with the post-operative challenges of pain. Those who attended this class reported that without the mindfulness practice, their control of pain would have been more challenging. Some even reported that they had no need to avail themselves of the prescribed opiates for the pain.

Prevents or Reduces Elevated Blood Pressure

Mindfulness practices are increasingly being used to prevent or reduce hypertension. One patient who came regularly to our mindfulness yoga classes was taking the vasodilator hydralazine (Apresoline) for her high blood pressure. Eventually her physician recommended that she lower the dosage of the medication because her blood pressure was reverting to normal levels. He attributed this to her routine practice of yoga, since the practice is known to lower blood pressure, probably due to an increase in antioxidants, which are known to lower the levels of cortisol.

Buffers Against Bullying

Children, teens, and young adults benefit tremendously from mindfulness training. We have noticed that children are less likely to have problems such as drinking alcohol, overeating, using drugs, and bullying others when taught how to meditate and practice mindfulness yoga.

We offer a yoga class for teenagers at our center. During a brainstorming session, a significant number of the children indicated that their favorite segment of the class was when they meditated in the corpse pose (*savasana*) position because "the pose helps us relax and helped us resist the pressure from older kids who try to get us to drink and smoke pot. It lets us realize that overeating and bullying others is not good. We now know what other kids are going through, especially the gay kids or the ones who do not speak English very well."

Just for fun, I asked a seven-year-old what pose she liked best, and to my surprise she responded the *garbhasana* (the fetal position) and the *kapotasana* (the pigeon pose). I said, "Wow, you've learned the names of the poses in Sanskrit!" To which she answered, "I know; that's because I'm gifted. In school, I'm in the advanced kids' program." As the saying goes, "Kids say the darndest things!"

Benefits College Students

The only mantra scientists and students often chant is: "Wait for the evidence. Is the evidence correct?" Therefore, getting students to buy into mindfulness has been no easy task. So, instead of getting them to learn how to avail themselves of the benefits of mindfulness, I alluded to using the term "attentiveness training."

Students who have come to our center have also experienced significant positive results by practicing the "attentiveness training" we teach. This includes a cohort of students from a local school who came to learn how to meditate before taking the standardized college admissions test (SAT). Although no outcome data was collected, anecdotally they reported that the training helped them with memory recall, concentration, and information processing.

Among the ones who have come to our center, one client studying for his License in Marriage and Family Therapy (LMFT) reported improvements in a wide range of areas, including improved concentration, enhanced problem-solving ability, sharpened memory recall, decreased reactivity, increased curiosity, improved patience and self-acceptance, and enhanced relational qualities. As a side benefit, he noted that he no longer consumes as much alcohol as he did before.

Boosts Resilience

In his study,[5] Dr. Shakya Kumara states, "Faced with pressure, challenge, and change, people's stress response can easily kick in, making them rigid, inflexible, and irritable. Sustained over time, the result is anxiety, depression, and burnout. This is a growing issue for us in the modern world. In the UK, for example, more than 50 percent of sick days are now due to such illnesses."

Resilience is the ability to respond well to difficulty. I helps maintain flexibility, constructive a ttitude, and positive mood, even under pressure. Mindfulness can help build up resilience in many ways.

Prevents Burnout and Compassion Fatigue

By integrating mindfulness in the workplace, we have been able to impact job performance in one of the hospitals in the area and reduce burnout, or what we call "compassion fatigue."

Additional benefits of the program included improved interaction between patient and healthcare providers, as well as among coworkers. Another benefit was increased productivity, with three of the participants indicating that *"they seemed to work less but get more done."* Analysis of the data showed enhanced morale; sharpened mental clarity; increased attentiveness, memory, and information processing; and improved impulse control.

Mindfulness Yoga Helps Children with Cerebral Palsy

In one study[6] the authors showed that their style of yoga, *MiYoga*, an embodied mindfulness-based movement program, enhanced attention (more attentive and consistent performance) in children with bilateral or unilateral cerebral palsy.

Enhances the Immune System

In a recent comprehensive review[7], which included data from 1,602 participants, tentative evidence revealed that mindfulness meditation is associated with changes in select biomarkers of immune system activity.

The i nvestigators o f t his r eview f ound t hat a cross t wenty randomized controlled trials (RTCs) and more than 1,600 participants, tentative evidence was found that mindfulness meditation modulates some select immune parameters in a manner that suggests a more *salutogenic* immune profile.

Specifically, mindfulness mediation appears to be associated with reductions in proinflammatory processes, increases in cell-mediated defense parameters, and increases in enzyme activity that guards against cell aging. Although these findings replicated and are based on well-designed RCTs, they are restricted to particular populations, subgroup analyses, and disease types. Consequently, additional research is needed to test the effects of mindfulness mediation on immune system biomarkers to provide a clearer understanding of the robustness and generalizability of findings, and to examine the relevance of these findings for clinical symptoms and overall health.

Helps with Anger Management

> "The first drawback of anger is that it destroys your inner peace; the second is that it distorts your view of reality. If you think about this and come to understand that anger is really unhelpful, that it is only destructive, then you can begin to distance yourself from anger."
>
> - Dalai Lama

Anger is an inevitable part of life, but blasting off on a frequent basis is not socially acceptable.

At our center, we offer mindfulness training in conjunction with life coaching to help those whose anger has gotten them into trouble with the law. Our intent is to help those who come to us take control and responsibility for themselves, learn to say "no" to unreasonable requests, eliminate the things that irritate them, set clear boundaries, and keep their anger and stress at acceptable levels.

Most of our clients are court-referred anger management cases, generally for an eight- to sixteen-week training program with two-hour sessions per week. We will inform the court when the anger management program has been completed, terminated, or extended and issue a document, which will include the credentials of the staff who provided the training.

Our clients learn to become familiar with the emotion of anger, learn compassion and empathy toward others, and learn how to respond rather than react to negative situations in a socially acceptable manner.

The anger management program we offer includes:

- Life coaching
- Sympathetic breathing
- Mind-body work (mindfulness yoga)
- Mindfulness of the thought patterns that feed the anger
- Identifying situations (triggers) that lead to anger
- Autogenics
- A diversity of mindfulness practices, such as mindful sitting, eating, and walking

Conclusion

Taken together, mindfulness offers us a cornucopia of benefits — from the reduction of stress to the management of psychological disorders, treating heart disease, lowering blood pressure, reducing chronic pain, improving sleep, and alleviating gastroin-testinal difficulties. M ndfulness ffects many aspects of our psychological well-being. These i nclude i mproving o ur m ood, increasing positive emotions, and decreasing our anxiety, emotional reactivity, and job burnout.

But most of all, mindfulness allows us to recognize that "All Lives Can't Matter Until Black Lives Matter."

5

BUT I DON'T HAVE TIME TO PRACTICE MINDFULNESS

"If you are taking a mindful walk, for example, you are not just getting from point A to point B. You are aware of and controlling your breathing. You are mindful of the nature around you and may be noticing things like leaves falling and animals playing. You are monitoring your thoughts, feelings, and body sensations."

~ Author unknown

*D*espite all of the benefits of mindfulness, the idea of taking five to ten minutes of silence from a busy schedule is something a lot of people find next to impossible. Plus, finding the right place to do so without the distraction of children or spouses can be difficult. On the other hand, not finding the time to take care of your mind and body is like saying, "I need to get to work, but I don't have time to put gas in the car."

Sometimes thinking about finding the time to meditate can become a point of stress. People find themselves rushing without time to relax and focus on what is happening in the present moment. When that happens, remember RAIN.[1]

- **R**ecognize what is going on – Consciously acknowledging, in any given moment, the thoughts, feelings, and behaviors that are affecting you.
- **A**llow the experience to be there, just as it is – Letting the thoughts, emotions, feelings, or sensations you have recognized to simply be there. Allowing creates a space that enables you to see more deeply into your own being, which, in turn, awakens your caring and helps you make wiser choices in life.
- **I**nvestigate with kindness – Investigating means calling on your natural curiosity, or if you will, the desire to know truth, and directing a more focused attention to your present experience.
- **N**atural awareness – This practice of non-identification means that your sense of who you are is not fused with any limiting emotions, sensations, or stories. You begin to intuit and live from the openness and love that express your natural awareness.

Another thing that you can do is take one of any activity of daily living and turn it into a mindfulness exercise — for example, brushing your teeth, washing dishes, bathing, or eating.

Mindful Eating Exercise

The one I am suggesting is eating. For this exercise you will need three small pieces of fruit (I suggest three raisins) or three small pieces of chocolate.

1. Start the exercise by becoming aware of your breath and your body. Plant your feet firmly on floor and notice how you feel at this very moment.
2. With your awareness in the now, notice any thoughts, feelings, or emotions you are experiencing. Notice whether or not you feel hungry, thirsty, or full.
3. What do you feel like eating of drinking at this very moment?
4. Proceed by paying attention to the item of food in front of you (three pieces of fruit or chocolate), imagining that it is the first time you see them. Notice their color, shape, texture, and size.
5. Now, think about what it took for these items of food to get to you — not only the forces of nature such as rain, sunshine, and earth but also the time it took for the food items to grow, the manpower involved, shipping, packing, and/or delivering them to the grocery store.
6. In your mind, express gratitude for everyone and everything involved in getting these items of food to you. If you say grace, this might be a good time to do so.
7. Now, pick up the first piece of food, place it between

your fingers, and feel the texture, temperature, and edges. Does it feel smooth, rough, sticky? Notice any thoughts, sensations, or emotions that crop up in your mind as you do this.

8. Be fully present as you continue to feel the piece of food. Then bring it toward your nose and smell it. What does it smell like? Does the aroma bring up any memories? Do you notice anything going on in your mouth or stomach as you smell the piece of food even before you put it in your mouth, such as increased salivation of gurgling in your stomach?

9. Proceed by bringing the piece of food up and placing it into your mouth without chewing or swallowing it. Just swirl it around with your tongue and allow it to be in your mouth for a while. What does it taste like? Notice its texture and flavor. What physical sensations are you noticing, especially in your mouth and your stomach?

10. Chew it slowly and swallow it. Now, notice that you are one piece of fruit or chocolate heavier!

11. Continue to breathe as you explore the sensation of having had this piece of fruit or chocolate.

12. Next, take the second piece of fruit or chocolate, place it in your mouth, and notice the flavor, the change in texture as you begin to swirl it around your mouth and chew it. Notice the little pieces of food in your mouth as you chew. Notice the sound, sensations, and the flavor of the food as you eat it.

13. When you are ready, swallow this second piece of food. Notice that it goes from your mouth, where it has been

digested in part by the salivary enzymes, down your throat, and into your stomach. Notice the taste and pieces that may hang around in your mouth and in between your teeth. Now you are two pieces of fruit or chocolate heavier!

14. Next, pick up the third piece of food and eat it whichever way you want. Just be aware of what you are experiencing as you eat this third piece.

15. Notice that it goes into your mouth where the teeth grind up the food and the salivary enzymes begin the process of digestion. Then down your throat, into the stomach where food is ground up even more, through the small intestine where the nutrients from the food are absorbed into your body, then into your large intestine, and eventually the residues are returned to the earth to serve as fertilizer for the growth of more food. And the cycle begins all over again.

Conclusion

Despite its benefits, the idea of taking time to practice mindfulness is something that many people find difficult. Also, finding the right time and place to do so in a formal way can be a problem.

Notwithstanding, there is a way of getting around this. Anything and everything you do can be done mindfully. Practice mindfulness during routine activities and soon you will be training the mind and changing the structure and function of your brain for the better. You can practice mindfulness while you are waiting, say in line to check out at the grocery store or at the post office. And before you know it, you will be taking advantage of all the benefits of mindfulness I have mentioned in Chapter 4.

Another activity that can be practiced mindfully is to pay close attention to your body as you simply walk (see Chapter 10).

6

TRAIN THE MIND, CHANGE THE BRAIN

"Do not call for black power or green power. Call for brain power."

~ Barbara Jordan

 W ith the regular practice of mindfulness, one can train the mind to experience living in such a way that one can empathize with the suffering of others.

Structural Changes in the Brain

The structural changes that take place in the brain, as a result of mindfulness practice, can be summed up by the work of Goleman and Davidson in their seminal work, *Altered Traits.*[1]

- The prefrontal cortex thickens, which is important for sensation, attention, self-regulation, the ability to anticipate the future, and manage reactivity. It guides behavior, inhibits the default area of the brain, controls worrying, and is entwined with emotional suffering.

- The insula thickens, which improves empathy and activates the automimic response (heart and breathing rates), increases blood flow to muscles, and attunes us to self-awareness.
- The somatomotor area thickens, which is the main area for sensing touch, pain, and bodily awareness.
- The anterior cingulate cortex thickens, which modulates inflammation, connects our thoughts and feelings, and controls autonomic activity, including heart and breathing rate.
- The orbitofrontal cortex thickens, which is also part of the circuitry for self-regulation.
- The amygdala shrinks, which is the trigger for the fight-flight-or-freeze area of the brain.

In addition to that, Mintie and Staples[2] found that the hippocampus, a node crucial for memory such as storing new memories and processing long-term memories, plays an important role in interacting with the amygdala during the encoding of emotional recollections.

Functional Changes in the Brain

Judson Brewer[3] in *The Craving Mind* has shown that, given its effects on the "self-control" regions of the brain, meditation can be remarkably effective in helping people recover from various types of addiction by the mere fact that the function of the brain changes in positive ways.

In fact, anyone who may be struggling to find the right treatment program for their addiction will find that mindfulness-based models offer a greater chance of success in achieving sobriety than the traditional twelve-step models.[4] However, the addicted individual must commit to practicing mindfulness routinely to succeed.

Readers interested in the details regarding the potential of the human mind should see Goleman and Davidson.[5] As one reviewer stated, "*Altered Traits* is your roadmap to a more mindful, compassionate, fulfilling life — and who doesn't want that?"

Vasovagal Activation

Cranial nerve X, the vagus nerve, extends from the brainstem down into the stomach and intestines, innervating the heart and lungs and connecting the throat and facial muscles. It regulates metabolic homeostasis by controlling the heart rate, gastrointestinal motility, gastric secretion of serotonin, pancreatic secretions, hepatic glucose production, as well as other endocrine and exocrine secretions.[6]

A properly functioning vagus nerve will improve brain-body communication and, in turn, make us feel much better. It is the nerve known for inducing loving kindness, intellectual fulfillment, and connection.

The best intervention for stimulating the vagus nerve is mindful, diaphragmatic breathing (also known as *eupnea*), which is done by contracting the diaphragm downward. In other words, by belly breathing. Air enters the lungs, the chest does not rise, and the belly expands outward. This recruits the parasympathetic nervous system.[7] The stimulation of the vagus occurs when the breath is slowed down from our typical ten to fourteen breaths per minute to five to seven breaths per minute. You can achieve this by counting the inhalation to five, holding the inbreath to a count of four, and exhaling to a count of eight or ten.

Vasovagal stimulation with mindfulness dramatically reduces the severity of depression. It also optimizes functional connectivity of the default mode network, which lowers inflammation and improves the brain's ability to manage stress and anxiety.[8]

Neuropeptide Modulation

During mindfulness meditation, when we sense that our environment is safe, the release of oxytocin, serotonin, dopamine, and endogenous opioids allows us to enjoy the comfort of "an embrace without fear." Coupled with that is a reduction in the levels of the stress hormones epinephrine, norepinephrine, and cortisol.[9]

Rick Hanson[10] has found that during mindfulness practice:

- Serotonin levels increase. Serotonin influences the regulation of mood, sleep, and digestion; most antidepressants aim at increasing its effects.
- Dopamine levels increase. This is the "feel-good" neuropeptide involved with reward and attention. It promotes approach behaviors. When the brain fails to produce enough dopamine, it can result in Parkinson's disease.
- Acetylcholine levels increase, promoting wakefulness

and learning. Acetylcholine is the neurotransmitter used at the neuromuscular junction, or, in other words, it is the chemical that motor neurons of the nervous system release in order to activate muscles. This property means that drugs that affect cholinergic systems can have extremely dangerous effects ranging from paralysis to convulsions.

- Endogenous opioid levels increase. These buffer the stress response, reduce pain, and produce pleasure (for example, the so-called "runner's high"); these include the endorphins and the endogenous analgesics.

- Oxytocin levels increase. Oxytocin is normally produced in the hypothalamus and released by the posterior pituitary and plays a role in social bonding, sexual reproduction, childbirth, and the period after childbirth. Promoting nurturing behaviors toward children and bonding in couples, oxytocin is associated with blissful closeness and love. Women produce more oxytocin than men.

- Vasopressin levels increase. Also known as the antidiuretic hormone, this endogenous peptide supports pair bonding. However, in men it may promote aggressiveness toward sexual rivals.

- Estrogen levels increase. The brains of both men and women contain estrogen receptors, which affects libido, mood, and memory.

- Dehydroepiandrosterone (DHEA ~ insulin-like growth factor)[11] also increases.

- Gamma-aminobutyric acid (GABA). "Best known for

making you feel calm, GABA is one of the major inhibitory neurotransmitters in your central nervous system. Anyone with an addiction, including alcohol, drugs, tobacco, caffeine, and food, all have one thing in common, which is a lack of GABA. Not having enough of this super-important chemical can create an array of problems, including anxiety, nervousness, racing thoughts, and sleeplessness. Luckily, there is an effective solution."[12]

"When these 'pleasure chemicals' surge into your synapses, they strengthen the neural circuits that are active, making them more likely to fire together in the future. Furthermore, busy neural networks receive increased blood flow, which supplies them with more glucose and oxygen."[13] That is, there is more blood flow to the thinking areas of the brain, thus information processing, memory recall, and learning are enhanced."

Electromagnetic Wave Signatures

During total absorption in undistracted concentration (*samadhi* in Sanskrit), an electromagnetic wave pattern is associated with a benign state of being.

In Richard Davidson's laboratory, brain waves were measured with what looks like a shower cap extruding spaghetti-like wires. This specially designed cap holds 256 thin wires, each leading to a sensor attached to a precise location on the scalp. A tight connection between the sensor and the scalp makes all the difference between recording usable data regarding the brain's electrical activity and having the electrode simply be an antenna for noise.[14]

- Alpha waves

In the early stages of meditation, there is an increase in alpha wave activity. This is associated with a state of relaxed wakefulness. There is also a greater synchronization of alpha wave activity across the two hemispheres. Behavioral studies have shown that greater synchrony between the two hemispheres is linked with both external attention and a lack of expectations.[15] This appears when we are doing little thinking and simply relaxing — a state of bare awareness, an effortless and brilliant state of rootless wisdom.

- Gamma Waves

Gamma, the very fastest brain wave, occurs during moments when differing brain regions fire in harmony, like moments of insight when different elements of a mental puzzle "click" together. This is the very wave that deep meditators display in that surprising surge during both open presence and compassion. It is the wave associated with loving kindness. The changes in gamma wave activity were much more pronounced in the experienced meditators than in a group of people who had been just taught how to meditate.[16]

- Delta Waves

Delta, the slowest wave, oscillates between one and four cycles per second, and occurs mainly during deep sleep.

- Theta Waves

Theta, the next slowest, can signify drowsiness.

According to van der Kolk in his seminal work *The Body Keeps the Score*[17], "Theta waves create a frame of mind unconstrained by logic or by the ordinary demands of life and thus open the potential for making novel connections and associations. One of the most promising EEG neurofeedback treatments for PTSD, alpha/theta training makes use of that quality to loosen frozen associations and facilitate new learning. On the downside, theta frequencies also occur when we're 'out of it' or 'depressed.'"

Conclusion

In this short chapter, I reiterate the fact that the regular practice of mindfulness allows one to train the mind to experience living in such a way that one can empathize with the suffering of others. It deracinates the ego from its infernal narcissism. Thus, I would like to end it with a poem I wrote a few years ago. [18]

Wounded Ego
When the ego feels
maimed or exploited,
nurture it,
acknowledging
your goodness and virtues.

When the ego feels
maimed or exploited,
nurture it as an infant
that needs cuddling and consoling,
acknowledging your goodness and virtues,
knowing that at any given moment
the soul is neither absolutely
sane nor insane.

Look for and exalt
the treasures within you, comprehending that
external validation
can be manipulative,
capricious,
or vain.

Yet, when the ego is exalted,
whence comes the exaltation?
From the need to quench
an untamable thirst for adulation…or from
a soul suffused
with the euphoria
of having touched a sprout
and seeing it bloom?

7
———

MINDFULNESS OF THE BREATH

"Breathe. Let go. And remind yourself that this very moment is the only one you know you have for sure."

~ Oprah Winfrey

Our bodies simply breathe on autopilot without our having to do anything. However, for years, it has been known that controlled breathwork — or pranayama, the fourth of Patanjali's eight limbs of yoga[1] — can be enormously powerful in altering the mind. It is by far one of the most effective ways to lower everyday stress levels and improve a variety of health factors ranging from mood to preventing relapse of episodes of depression.[2] And of course, it is a way of helping us identify with the suffering of others, as well as understand our own misgivings or self-assurance. It is a way of understanding that "All Lives Can't Matter Until Black Lives Matter."

Notwithstanding the inherently automatic nature of the breath, most of us have much to learn about this basic physiological mechanism. Normally, the human being takes approximately fourteen to twenty breaths per minute.[3]

Activation of the Sympathetic Nervous System

With rapid breathing or hyperventilation, millions of sensory receptors in the respiratory system send signals via the vagus nerve to the brainstem. With each rapid inbreath, the sympathetic nervous system is activated and

- there is an increase in the secretion of the stress hormones (cortisol, epinephrine, and norepinephrine);
- the heart rate increases;
- blood pressure rises;
- muscles tense up;
- sweat production increases; and
- anxiety levels go up.

Recruitment of the Parasympathetic Nervous System

On the other hand, slowing down your breathing recruits the parasympathetic nervous system, dialing down all of the above, inducing relaxation, serenity, and as I said before, the ability to identify with the suffering of others, as well as understand our own misgivings and uncertainties.

Soft-Belly Breathing

According to James Gordon, MD,[4] scientists have shown that by meditating regularly, particularly by practicing "soft belly " breathing, you increase the functioning of the vagus nerve. And with better vagal functioning, you get better self-regulation, enhanced memory, clearer thinking, greater ability to deal with life's stresses, and quicker recovery from anger and distress. The improved vagal tone that comes with controlled breathing also activates the nerves associated with facial expression and speech, which makes it easier for us to recognize and welcome the support that others may want to give. Meditation enhances functioning in the hippocampus, a crucial structure for quieting agitation and consolidating memory. Meditation actually promotes the growth of new brain tissue in areas of the frontal cortex that trauma often damages — areas responsible for self-awareness, thoughtful judgment, and compassion.

The "Soft-Belly" Breathing Technique of James Gordon

1. Sit or lie down in a comfortable position in a space where you will not be disturbed. Turn off your phone and, if you wish, turn on some soft background music.
2. Gently close your eyes or, if you wish, you may keep them open. Take your mind to your nostrils and start noticing your inbreath and your outbreath.
3. Proceed by letting your mind go to your abdomen, and as you inhale say to yourself "soft," and notice how your abdomen and/or torso inflate. As best you can, try to direct your breath to the abdomen.
4. Then as you breathe out, say "belly."
5. Continue the exercise for fifteen to twenty minutes.

Remember that during exhalation, parasympathetic nerve activity in the vagus nerve also increases, causing the heart rate to slow, while the opposite occurs during inhalation.

Two-Line Directional Breathing Exercise

The benefits of this exercise are remarkably similar to those of the "soft-belly" breathing.

1. Begin by lying down on your back, preferably on a soft surface such as your bed or a mat. You may use a small pillow under your head and a bolster under your knees, or even a folded blanket or towel beneath your lumbar area for support. You may also roll up a towel or blanket to place under your ankles for support.

2. Rest your arms along the side of your body, not touching the body, palms up preferably if that is comfortable for you. Your heels should be two feet to two and a half feet apart with the ankles rotating comfortably outwards.

3. Begin by taking your mind to your nostrils and proceed with a minute or so of "soft-belly" breathing to bring the mind to the present moment.

4. After the mind has calmed down, draw an imaginary line that extends from the tip of your nose, down through your navel, all the way down to the pubis, so that your torso is divided into a right and left side.

5. Now, notice which side you are breathing more efficiently into, the right or the left? This varies from person to person.

6. Continue breathing into that space for a few minutes, gently but firmly bringing the mind right back to the breath if it has drifted into the past or into the future.

7. Now, take in a deep breath to inflate your lungs to the fullest, hold it to a count of four or so, and let it out slowly through your mouth.

8. Intentionally, start breathing into the other side. That is, if you were breathing more efficiently into the left side, switch your breathing to the right, or vice versa.

9. Continue breathing into that space for a few minutes. And as before, gently but firmly bringing the mind right back to the breath if it has drifted into the past or into the future.

10. After you have breathed for a few minutes, take in a deep breath to inflate your lungs to the fullest, hold it to a count of four or so, and let it out slowly though your mouth.

11. This time draw an imaginary line that divides the torso into an upper half and a lower half. That would be a horizontal line approximately two inches above the navel. Notice which side you are breathing more efficiently into, the upper or the lower half? Again, this varies from person to person.

12. Continue breathing into that space for a few minutes, gently but firmly bringing the mind back to the breath if it has wandered from the present moment.

13. Again, take in a deep breath to inflate your lungs to the fullest, hold it to a count of four or so, and let it out slowly though your mouth.

14. Now, consider both lines, the horizontal and the vertical. Taken together they divide the torso into four quadrangles — two upper and two lower. Notice which quadrangle you are breathing more efficiently into, remembering that this varies from person to person.

15. Continue breathing into that quadrangle for a few minutes, gently but firmly bringing the mind back to the breath if it has wandered from the present moment.

16. Take in a deep breath to inflate your lungs to the fullest, hold it to a count of four or so, and let it out slowly though your mouth.

17. This time intentionally breathe into the diagonally opposite quadrangle. That is, if you were breathing more efficiently into the upper right, direct your breath to the lower left.

18. Continue breathing into that quadrangle for a few minutes.

19. Now, play a game with yourself. Start switching from quadrangle to quadrangle, directing a couple of breaths into one quadrangle then switching to another. You may do this clockwise, counterclockwise, or randomly.

20. After you have done this for a few minutes, take in a deep breath to inflate your lungs to the fullest, hold it to a count of four or so, and let it out slowly though your mouth.

21. Let your breath return to normal.

22. At this time, I invite you to let your mind go to your feet. Imagine little openings on the soles of your feet. Let your mind go to the crown of your head and

imagine an opening on the crown of your head about one inch in diameter.

23. Using your imagination, envision breathing in through your feet, imagine the breath rush up your legs, your pelvis, your torso, your neck, and when the breath gets into your head, expel it out through the imaginary opening on the crown of your head. Imagine getting rid of all the toxins in your body, breathing in fresh oxygenated air, flushing out all negativity that is within you — no need to identify it, just get rid of it.

24. And if you wish, you may reverse the direction of breathing — inhaling through the crown of your head and exhaling through the soles of your feet.

25. When you are ready, you may bring sensation back into the body by wiggling your fingers, your toes, bringing your arm overhead and stretching, and pointing and flexing your feet.

26. To get up safely, grab the right knee with both hands and pull it tightly into the chest, then put it down.

27. Do the same thing with the left knee.

28. Then grab both knees, bring them into the chest, and gently start rocking side to side.

29. Eventually rock all the way to the left, form a little pillow under your head with your left arm, and rest there for a brief moment.

30. When you are ready to get up, stretch your top leg downward. Place your right hand on the floor in front of your chest and, applying pressure with the right arm, come to a seated position.

31. Now briskly rub the palms of your hands together to generate some heat. If you wear glasses, take them off. Then cover your eyes with your hands and enjoy the warmth.

32. Take a few moments to notice how you feel and to congratulate yourself for taking the time to take care of yourself.

Lobes of the Lung Directional Breathing Exercise

1. As with the previous exercise, lie down on your back, preferably on a soft surface such as your bed or a mat. Use a small pillow under your head and a bolster under your knees, if you wish, or even a folded blanket or towel beneath your lumbar area for support. You may also roll up a towel or blanket to place under your ankles for support.

2. Rest your arms along the side of your body, not touching the body, palms facing upwards preferably if that is comfortable for you. Your heels should be two feet to two and a half feet apart with the ankles rotating comfortably outwards.

3. Begin by taking your mind to your nostrils and proceed with a minute or so of "soft-belly " breathing to bring the mind to the present moment.

4. After the mind has calmed down, remembering that the right lung has three lobes and the left two, let your mind go to the lower right rib cage, about two inches below the level of your navel,

and start directing your breath into that area of your body.

5. Notice how the lower right side of your abdomen (your belly) expands outwards with the inhale and retracts with the exhale.

6. Continue breathing into that space for a few minutes, gently but firmly bringing the mind right back to the breath if it has drifted into the past or into the future.

7. Now, take in a deep breath to inflate your lungs to the fullest, hold it to a count of four or so, and let it out slowly though your mouth.

8. Intentionally, let your mind go to the middle of the right rib cage, about three inches of so above the level of your navel, at the lower end of the rib cage, and start directing your breath into that area of your body.

9. Notice how the midsection of your abdomen and rib cage expand outwards with the inhale and retract with the exhale.

10. Continue breathing into that space for a few minutes, remembering to gently but steadfastly bring the mind right back to the breath if it has wandered elsewhere.

11. Proceed by letting your mind go to your right upper torso, the right shoulder, and notice how the shoulder goes up with the inbreath and down with the outbreath.

12. Stay there for a few minutes.

13. Again, remembering that the left lung two has two lobes, let your mind go to the lower left rib cage, about two inches below the level of your navel, right below

the left rib cage, and start directing your breath into that area of your body.

14. Continue breathing into that space for a few minutes.

15. Now, let your mind go to your let upper torso, the left shoulder, and notice how the shoulder elevates with the inbreath and descends with the outbreath.

16. After a few minutes, take in a deep breath to inflate your lungs to the fullest, hold it to a count of four or so, and let it out slowly though your mouth.

17. Let your breath return to normal.

18. At this time, I invite you to let your mind go to your feet. Imagine little openings on the soles of your feet. Let your mind go to the crown of your head and imagine an opening on the crown of your head about one inch in diameter.

19. Using your imagination, envision breathing in through your feet, imagining the breath rush up your legs, your pelvis, your torso, your neck, and when the breath gets into your head, expel it out through the imaginary opening on the crown of your head. Imagine getting rid of all the toxins in your body, breathing in fresh oxygenated air, flushing out all negativity that is within you — no need to identify it, just get rid of it.

20. And if you wish, you may reverse the direction of breathing — inhaling through the crown of your head and exhaling through the soles of your feet.

21. When you are ready, you may bring sensation back into the body by wiggling your fingers, your toes, bringing

your arm overhead and stretching, and pointing and flexing your feet.

22. If you have been doing the exercise lying on your back, to get up safely, grab the right knee with both hands and pull it tightly into the chest, then put it down.

23. Do the same thing with the left knee.

24. Then grab both knees, bring them up towards your chest, and gently start rocking side to side.

25. Eventually rock all the way to the left, form a little pillow under your head with your left arm, and rest there for a brief moment.

26. When you are ready to get up, stretch your top leg downward. Place your right hand on the floor in from of your chest and, applying pressure with the right arm, come to a seated position.

27. Now briskly rub the palms of your hands together to generate some heat. If you wear glasses, take them off. Then cover your eyes with your hands and enjoy the warmth.

28. Take a few moments to notice how you feel and to congratulate yourself for taking the time to take care of yourself.

Matter **Three Minute Breathing Space Exercise**

1. Awareness

Bring yourself into the present moment by deliberately adopting an erect and dignified posture. If possible, close your eyes. Then ask:

"What is my experience right now...in thoughts...in emotions...and in bodily sensations?"

Acknowledge and register your experience, even if it is unwanted.

2. Gathering

Then, gently redirect full attention to breathing, to each inbreath and to each outbreath as they follow, one after the other.

Your breath can function as an anchor to bring you into the present and help you tune into a state of awareness and stillness.

3. Expanding

Expand the field of your awareness around your breathing so that it includes a sense of the body as a whole, your posture, and facial expression.

The breathing space provides a way to step out of autopilot mode and reconnect with the present moment.

The key skill in practicing *mindfulness* is to maintain awareness in the moment. Nothing else.

Conclusion

Remember the power of the breath. Always, and as best you can, try to focus on diaphragmatic breathing (belly breathing) since it regulates the sympathetic nervous system, causing the parasympathetic nervous system to become dominant.

On the other hand, shallow breathing, holding your breath, and hyperventilating triggers the sympathetic nervous system into a "fight/flight/freeze" response.

And certainly, controlled breathing helps us enjoy the vividness and exquisiteness available to us in the present moment. It allows us to be aware of the agony and anguish of those who are different and less fortunate from us, as well as help us understand the chaos and bliss within us.

8

MINDFULNESS ON OUR DOMAINS OF BEING

"All mankind... being all equal and independent, no one ought to harm another in his life, health, liberty, or possessions."

~ John Locke

The domains of the human being are often defined as the physical, psychological, social, and spiritual ambits of life. However, for our purpose, I define these as our health and well-being, creativity, stability, loving kindness, and a fifth domain which I have added — our nothingness or self-lessness.

Borrowing from Dr. Dolores Seymour's course MINDS,[1] from the American Institute of Holistic Health & Wellness, this mindfulness intervention, which she calls "The Golden Castle," begins with a visit through a golden castle by the ocean.

First Domain — Health and Well-Being

None of us enjoy what we would call perfect health. We are born, we live, and eventually, due to disease, suicide, homicide, or an accident, we die — our physical body rushes forth to the unknown. We are here on this planet but for a blink of an eye. Some say, "We only live once." Others say, "We only die once." Whether you prefer the former or the latter, the fact is that the only time to be happy is now — not yesterday nor tomorrow.

So, let us begin our imaginary journey and explore our domains of being.

Sit or lie calmly and comfortably on your back. Imagine yourself walking along a white, sandy beach on a bright sunny day carrying a large wicker basket strapped onto your back with leather straps with all of your *negativity* within it. All of a sudden and unexpectedly, you see a shovel on the ground. You pick it up, dig a large, deep hole, and bury all of your dark cloud of negativity in it — without any need for identifying any of it; you just simply bury it.

Then you proceed to walk up the steps of a castle. You open its massive wooden front doors, carved with figures of lions and arches, and proceed to walk through the castle's inner hallway. As you do so, you listen to the imaginary sounds of the ocean waves crashing upon limestone ledges, seagulls fighting over a piece of discarded picnic bread, and the sound of an imaginary foghorn in the distance. You feel the soft, plush carpeting beneath your bare feet as you come to a variety of rooms decorated with furnishings of different colors. As you come to the first one, the

"Red Room," all furnished in red, you carefully open the door and take your time looking at everything in the room. From the furniture to the paintings on the wall, the ceiling chandelier and the red end-table lamps — all is red.

As you look at the furnishings in the room, bearing in mind that most of us don't enjoy perfect health, you focus on those aspects of the *good health* and *vitality* you relish — your ability to move, to feed yourself; that is, your ability to carry out your activities of daily living.

Doing so, you envision anything you enjoy that is red — the red of a gorgeous American Beauty red rose; the reds of an early morning sunrise or evening sunset splashed across the sky; or a field of early-spring, red poppies bathed by the rays of an early morning sunrise.

Second Domain — Creativity

Slowly, you leave the Red Room, lock the door behind you, and proceed as you did before, listening to the imaginary sounds, sights, and sensations around you — the portraits of royalty along the walls, or the make-believe beautiful, French, beige-colored windows—until you come to the "Blue Room," with sparkling blue furnishings. As you view the room, you contemplate and think about your *creativity* — your ability to read, write, solve problems, follow instructions. Perhaps you have a special talent in a particular area, let's say playing an instrument, writing poetry or prose, or you are great at mechanics. Bring to mind any shade, tone, or hue of blue of something that you enjoy — the light blue of the mid-morning sky, the aquamarine of oceans or beaches you have visited, a bowl of wild blue berries, a beautiful blue hydrangea, or a pair of alluring, piercing blue eyes.

Third Domain — Stability

You turn around, gently close the door of the Blue Room behind you, and continue as you did before, listening, seeing, and feeling all of the imaginary sights, sounds, and sensations until you come to another door labeled the "Green Room." You open the door and see that everything is furnished in green. Through an open door you even see a bedroom with a canopy bed dressed in green bedding. This time you think about the *stability* in your life — your ability to live within your means, to respond rather than react to a situation, or to end a bad relationship. All in all, most of us have good days and bad days, but taken together, our lives are relatively stable. So, as you think of the stability you enjoy, think of any tone, shade, or hue of green of something you enjoy — the color of pristine woods you have walked through; the greenery of mountains in the early spring; a soft, grassy meadow; or a tasty, luscious avocado you are about to peel.

Fourth Domain — Loving Kindness

Proceeding as you did before, you softly close the door of the Green Room and continue walking down the hallway, savoring the imaginary sounds, sights, and sensations until you come to the "White Room." You open the door and see that all décor is white. You look at the furnishings, the couch, coffee table, carpet — everything is white. And you feel all of the *loving kindness* within you — toward yourself, your loved ones, friends, those who are different from you, strangers you meet at the grocery store or the post office, adversaries, pets, animals, and all living beings on the surface of our planet. As you do so, you imagine things of any tone, shade, or hue of white that you love — a snow-covered mountain in early winter; a white, sandy beach you have visited; a snowman you have built with your children; a white owl surreptitiously glancing behind the beams of an old barn; or a white, puffy cloud on a bright summer day. And you say to yourself, "Yes, All Lives Can't Matter Until Black Lives Matter."

Fifth Domain — Nothingness

Now I invite you to continue walking down the central, grand hallway of the castle and, alluding to your imagination, keep on envisioning the sights and sounds of the ocean waves crashing against the rocks, the caws of the seagulls, and feeling the soft carpeting oozing in between your toes. You continue walking toward the room that I have invented, the "Colorless Room." You open the door and see nothing but an empty room and wonder. There is nothing in that room! It is empty! What you see is your soul, that empty space within you where everything exists.[2]

Yes, that's right, you see nothing because we are nothing but "little explosions of pretentiousness in the big gutter of humanity." We are selfless; there is neither superiority nor inferiority, no black-skinned or white-skinned people, there is no racial injustice, no white supremacy, and no discrimination. Again, I reiterate there is no such thing as "race." "All Lives Can't Matter Until Black Lives Matter."

Over and over I emphasize the fact that we all descend from the same maternal womb, that we are born, we live, and eventually we evanesce to realms unknown. We are here but for an imperceptible moment. Perhaps you have photographs at home of relative that are no longer with you. Look at them and recognize our ephemerality.

Accordingly, as you think of our *nothingness*, perhaps you'd like to bring to mind any tone, shade, or hue of something that is colorless that you like — a thought that enters and leaves your awareness in a split second, a dream that inspired you to write a poem or extend loving kindness to a friend or love one, a glass of cool refreshing water to quench your thirst, a windowpane through which you can look out at an early-evening sunset painted from the palette of Nature, the awareness of warm sand beneath your bare feet as you walk along the beach, or the mystery and miracle of your ability to think.

Conclusion

Our ambits of reality — our health and vitality, creativity, stability, ability to express loving kindness, and especially our egalitarianism — define who we are as human beings. They are domains that surpass the traditional definition of the psychological, social, and spiritual dimensions of life. Unlike what our current administration predicates, let's not forget — and I keep echoing — that we were born to be happy, make others happy, and alleviate the suffering of those who suffer.

To conclude, I would like to finish t his c hapter with a s mall poem I wrote several years ago that shows how we can easily miss our inner greatness if we fail to look within ourselves with a clear mind.

Dusty Mirror[3]

Dark gloomy morning
adumbrating unfulfilled promises.

Crusty eyes, evading the reality of
the breath of merciful winds.

On a mirror
covered with fine,
greyish dust
reflects a pathetic,
forlorn face.

What would that face look like
on a dusted and polished mirror?

9
_____

THE SCIENCE OF WESTERN YOGA

"Yoga does not just change the way we see things, it transforms the person who sees."

~ BKS Iyengar

*I*n 1893, Swami Vivekananda gave several lectures at the Chicago World Parliament of Religions. The event effectively marked the start of yoga in the United States and the birth of modern yoga as a transnational movement. It was followed in 1896 by his popular book, *Raja Yoga & Patanjali Yoga Sutra.*[1]

It is remarkably interesting how people consider the word "yoga." Epistemologically, from Sanskrit, *yoga* means union with the all-pervading energy of the Divine to achieve Bliss. Or if you will, the union of the body with the spirit — the true self.

As we practice it in the West, as Gary Kraftsow indicates,[2] yoga prepares us to confront death with a sense of gratitude and peace.

First and foremost, yoga encompasses more than the asanas (the postures and movements of the body). Yoga allows us to recognize our true nature. The practice allows us to integrate emotions and spirituality so that the mind (*Citta*) becomes consciousness (*Citi*).

At our center, we base our practice of yoga on science and neurobiological facts, not on esoteric, mythological, spiritual, mystical, metaphorical, or ritualistic ideals such as vestments, jewelry, or sculptures.

In my opinion, the aim of the yoga teacher is to have the student:

- Prepare for the end of life with a sense of appreciation and tranquility.
- Understand the purpose and meaning of life.
- Decrease suffering.
- Connect with the Divine.
- Understand their multidimensional nature.
- Recognize that the asanas have little value of their own. They are a way of cultivating the relationship between the breath with parts of the body, especially the spine, head, and neck so as to improve cardiac, liver, and kidney function, strengthen the immune system, notice thoughts as they enter and leave the mind, and recognize the impermanence of all phenomena.
- Establish neuromuscular reeducation.

- Establish sympathetic-parasympathetic regulation.
- Cope with chronic states of anxiety or depression — mental illness.
- Recognize the science of singing and chanting. That it is a way of learning, changing your mood, creating a deeper meaning, and lengthening the breath. (The teacher must be trained in doing this.)
- Learn the science of meditation; learn to respect it — know that it influences the way you see yourself, empty yourself of yourself.
- Learn how to reach your highest potential.
- Cultivate power and energy.
- Link the mind with their spirit and love toward themselves and others.
- Learn that "All Lives Can't Matter Until Black Lives Matter."

Tantra Yoga

All disciplines of yoga have passed through the tradition of Tantra. A lot of misunderstanding exists about Tantra Yoga, especially in the West, which recognizes Tantra as rituals engaged in uninhibited sex. Unfortunately, in the Western world, Tantra has been so poorly misinterpreted. This is so because Tantric literature has been written by people interested in selling books. Yogi Sadhguru explains what Tantra really is and what it is not.[3]

The word "Tantra" literally means "loom, warp, or weave," a word that also appears in the hymns of the Rigveda with the meaning of "warp" (weaving).[4]

Tantra recognizes that the human being is a composite of the physical body, a buildup of the food we consume, the mind (the brain that allows us to function in specific ways), and the energy body (the fundamental upon which the body and the mind are housed).

The simple tenet of Tantra Yoga is: "That the ways in which a man or woman usually pursues life is through food, alcoholic drink, and sex." Tantra Yoga uses these three domains to elevate consciousness. Tantra is about building our energies to attain consciousness of who we are.

Trauma-Sensitive Yoga

Another form of yoga that is important, especially for those suffering from PTSD or C-PTSD, is Trauma-Sensitive Yoga, inmoved by David Emerson at the Trauma Center of the Justice Research Institute in Needham, Massachusetts.[5]

In brief, this style of yoga derives from van der Kolk's work[6] in which he shows that patients who have suffered from emotional trauma present with depersonalization, or the outward symptoms of the *freeze* response, including the characteristic blank stare, shortness of breath, increased heart rate, sweating, and choking. The patient, instead of struggling to flee, lose their interoception (the signaling and perception of internal bodily sensations) to protect themselves. This sort of immobilization is generated in the reptilian brain of the most chronically traumatized persons. The aim of this style of yoga is to get the patient to regain sensation in the "frozen" areas of the body. Once sensation is regained, the patient begins to recover.

Yoga Nidra

Yoga Nidra induces the yogi (client) into a state of consciousness between waking and sleeping — a state in which the body is completely relaxed, yet the yogi can follow verbal instructions and cues from the teacher.

This style we teach our clients was innovated by Richard Miller, Ph.D.[7] During the practice, we encourage the client to notice the somatic, visceral, and kinesthetic sensations, the breath, and emotions felt during the exercise.

Before the exercise begins, the client is invited to recall and explore a positive, euphoric event experience in the past and try to recall everything about that event. For example, the client is encouraged to recall as much as possible about the event, such as the time the event occurred, the other people present at the time, expressions on their faces, the clothing worn, emotions felt then and now, etc. The client is encouraged to chat with the event. "Please, tell me more, I want to know as much as possible about what happened that day."

The client is even asked to give the event a number on a scale of pleasure ranging from one to ten, with ten being the most euphoric, or giving it a color.

After a few minutes of exploring the euphoric event, the client is invited to recall and explore a catastrophic, negative, traumatic, or embarrassing event experienced in the past.

Similarly, the client is encouraged to recall as much as possible about the negative event — the time it occurred, the place, if any other people were present at the time, expressions on their faces, the clothing worn, emotions felt at the time and now, etc. The client is invited to talk to the event. "Tell me more, I want to know more about what happened."

The instructor keeps switching back and forth between the positive and negative event for about five or six times, then rings a bell and brings the client back to the present moment.

The purpose of the exercise is to allow the participant to delve into how the mind handles and modulates events experienced in the past and how such events impact their well-being in the present moment — recognizing that the positive and negative counterbalance each other.

This exercise is particularly beneficial for clients who have suffered a traumatic event in the past. This would include PTSD or Complex Post-Traumatic Stress Disorder (C-PTSD). C-PTSD is a closely related condition to PTSD, which is becoming more widely recognized by mental health professionals. The disorder results from repeated trauma over months or years rather than from a single event, such as sexual abuse. These clients soon begin to recognize that the past is unchangeable and indefatigable and need not intrude into or impact on the vividness and exquisiteness available to them in the present moment.

Testimonials

PTSD

This is a statement from a client who suffered from PTSD as a result of a gunshot wound to the chest during a shootout at a night club. To show his dramatic improvement, the final session was to guide him thorough the Yoga Nidra exercise during which he relived the evening of the shooting.

I am Ivan,* a twenty-nine-year-old single male, who first came to see Dr. Casellas following a shooting at a night club where I suffered a gunshot wound to the chest. As a result of the incident, I developed PTSD. At the time I was under the care of a psychiatrist who had prescribed medication for my classic symptoms of PTSD which included nightmares, upsetting memories, physical reactivity after exposure to traumatic reminders, insomnia, flashbacks, severe anxiety, and depression.

During our first session, I spent over forty-five minutes talking nonstop about the severe trauma that had caused me so much emotional and physical pain. I was reliving and relating everything that happened that evening, from the moment I was shot, to when a policeman painfully inserted a finger into the wound to stop the bleeding, to being transported by ambulance to the hospital, to the moment when I passed out, thinking I had died.

When I finished talking, I remember Dr. Casellas looking into my eyes and saying, "Ivan, I'm so sorry for what you've experienced and I'm so glad you survived that horrible incident. But let me be honest; what you have been telling me is a story of something that happened in the past. What we are going to be working on is learning how to let go of the past and start living in the present moment, because the past is over and done with; it is unchangeable and indefatigable. I am going to attempt to teach you how to enjoy the vividness and exquisiteness that's available to you in the now and recognize, as my mentor once told me, 'as long as we are breathing, there is more right with us than there is wrong.'"

Over the next several weeks I met with Dr. Casellas once a week, learning the various mindfulness interventions of parasympathetic breathing, eating mindfully, walking meditation, autogenics, Yoga Nidra, the classic body scan, and loving kindness meditation. I was also provided with audio links to practice mindfulness before going to bed at night and upon waking in the morning.

As I felt safer, my fears and rages began to subside. There was in me something that was real. However, over the New Year's holiday I stopped going to the center.

After several months had passed, I reached out to Dr. Casellas again because my symptoms had exacerbated. I had stopped practicing the interventions he had taught me. It had reached the point that I quit my dreams of becoming an attorney after I failed my midterm exams due to depression and anxiety. I had experienced rapid weight gain and was avoiding all social interactions by not leaving my house if at all possible. I even resorted to sleeping with a loaded gun under my pillow "just in case."

When Dr. Casellas agreed to see me again, I restarted practicing the interventions and doing the homework assignment of mediating every day with the audio links he provided. I also used each meal as an opportunity to get my mind out of the default *daydreaming mode, back into the present moment to escape the trap of focusing on the past. I shared my excitement with him and spoke about moments of irritability and anger that, until recently, would have sent me into a rage that would last for hours, with negative thoughts filling my mind, leaving me hopeless.*

All of this changed with the meditation techniques I was practicing daily with a scented candle to help me focus on the aroma as I meditated. While controlling my breathing, I would picture a red ball in the center of my brain (the amygdala) capturing the anger and shrinking.

I also practiced the supine parasympathetic breathing intervention using the Inner Balance Application[8], an app that uses a sensor that clips onto the earlobe and another the center of the chest. When connected to a cell phone, the app displays the coherence level as it helps one concentrate on the breathing. Using the app, I was able to maintain high levels of coherence (99 percent) after ten minutes of parasympathetic breathing.

Finally, Dr. Casellas guided me through the Yoga Nidra exercise during which I used the night of the shooting as the negative, catastrophic event. To my surprise, I was able to complete the exercise successfully. I successfully relived the night of the shooting, the policeman sticking his finger in the wound to stop the bleeding, as well as the trip in the ambulance.

I am now able to focus on my physical recovery after having established a daily routine for my mental health. I am studying to retake the Law School Admission Test (LSAT) in hopes of joining a tier-one law school. I still have flashbacks and nightmares, but I don't let these define me. Through mindfulness, I am able to overcome these obstacles and concentrate on being the overachieving law student I once was.

Dr. Casellas, thanks for giving me a new lease on life." ~ I.S.

C-PTSD

This second testimonial is from a client who suffered repeated sexual abuse as a child from her uncle and was diagnosed as suffering from the complex from of Post-Traumatic Stress (C-PTSD).

Sherry,* a forty-six-year-old female, was brought to our center by her husband, Rick, seeking relief for the nightmares, flashbacks, insomnia, anxiety, depression, and dissociation she was experiencing as a result of being sexually abused by her uncle when she was a child. She was under the care of a psychiatrist who prescribed medication for her C-PTSD and insomnia. In addition to the psychological disorders, Sherry suffers from an autoimmune condition, congestive obstructive pulmonary disease (COPD), for which she uses a portable oxygen supply.

Sherry had never heard of or practiced mindfulness or any other form of meditation.

During the initial interview, Sherry cried as she voiced the history of the abuse by her uncle, as well as sharing the fact that she was married to Rick who would "take advantage of her against her will" at night with a loaded gun on the bedside table while she was under the effect the of medication her psychiatrist had prescribed. As such, she could not defend herself against Rick. She indicated that she loved Rick, would do anything for him, and wanted to save the marriage. I told her the fact she was "being taken advantage of sexually against her will at gunpoint" was not acceptable and that goals had to be set to remedy the situation. Any sexual interaction with her husband was to be a mutually consensual and enjoyable experience.

Throughout the course of management, she was taught Trauma-Sensitive Yoga (the TSY discussed in Chapter 4), sympathetic breathing, eating meditation, autogenics, walking meditation, and loving kindness meditation. The TSY revealed loss of sensation in her pelvic and thoracic areas She was also provided with audio recordings to practice the meditations at home and the recording of "The Golden Castle" by Dolores Seymour, Ph.D.[9] The interventions she preferred were the walking and eating meditation, "The Golden Castle" recording, and a recording of a sympathetic breathing meditation I recorded for her.

After the first session, Sherry said:
"You know, I believe you're going to help me save my marriage."

However, the marriage could not be saved. Rick, who was not contributing much to the household income, continued abusing her sexually against her will and draining the household budget. Sherry got an attorney who filed a restraining order against Rick and eventually helped Sherry divorce him. Within a few months after the divorce, her improvement was an extraordinary success story, as expressed in her own words:

*"Dr. Casellas, your private sessions have
helped me more than you'll ever know. You have helped me
find inner peace while struggling with my disorder not only
during my divorce but in coping with the flashbacks and
nightmares. I have many things to be grateful for. I am
finding ways of letting go of the past and being in the present
moment. I've grown to appreciate you and your teachings so
much. I am so grateful. I am now able to get back to my art,
write poetry, and I have even established an online store."*

She has authored a self-published, coffee-table book with poems and
paintings she has titled Impressions of Sunrises.

This is one of her poems, which shows her keen ability to observe,
which is an attribute that I consider the highest form of intelligence.

Dawn[10]

*The crescent moon fades
as a golden melody
graces the morning sky
with strokes of pink and purple
tones anticipating
a crescendo of light;
one ray, then two.
The wistful wind whistles the
humid air wrestling
an orchestra of clouds
back and forth, to the beat like
notes playing on a tapestry a
beam strums the lining silver*

while others radiate through
the shadows gold;
keeping temp to the wind.

The sun caresses the horizon glistening
across the salty waves crashing on shore,
like a symphony embracing the earth.

* The names of the clients have been changes to protect their identity.

10

LOVING KINDNESS

"We all are so deeply interconnected; we have no option but to love all. Be kind and do good for any one and that will be reflected. The ripples of the kind heart are the highest blessings of the Universe."

~ Amit Ray

*M*aitrī (Sanskrit: mettā) means loving kindness, an active interest in yourself, your loved ones, friends, strangers, all other living things, and even those who cause you difficulties — adversaries, foes, and enemies.

The cultivation of *loving kindness* comprises one of the four immeasurables in the Brahmavihara ("abodes of Brahma") of Buddhism.

The other three include *compassion* (karuna), *e mpathetic joy* (mudita) or joy for the achievement of others, and *equanimity* (upekṣā/upekkha) or, if you will, composure or self-discipline.

Those who practice the Brahmavihara, the Four Qualities of Love as described by Thích Nhat Hanh, recognize our homogeneity and that "All Lives Can't Matter Until Black Lives Matter."[1]

- May all beings enjoy happiness and the roots of happiness.
- May all beings be free from suffering and the roots of suffering.
- May they never be separated from the great joy, devoid of suffering.
- May they dwell in equanimity free from passion, aggression, and prejudice.

We practice loving kindness primarily because it serves as a necessary and potent antidote to ill will and inhumanity. We must avoid succumbing to all kinds of discrimination — Negrophobia, Hispanophobia, Islamophobia, anti-Semitism, Atheophobia, misogyny, ableism (discrimination against the handicapped), homo-aversion, transphobia, sectarianism (discrimination against a particular sect, especially religious ones), and all kinds of feelings of superiority or phobias against those who are different. We need to feel like we belong — a place where we can breathe and share our own story, so that we can remember that "All Lives Can't Matter Until Black Lives Matter."

An Exercise on Metta — Loving Kindness

This is an exercise of bestowing loving kindness onto yourself, a loved one, a friend, a stranger, someone who causes you difficulties, and all living beings on the universe. It is based on the one taught at the Center for Mindfulness in Medicine, Healthcare, and Society at the University of Massachusetts School of Medicine by Jon Kabat-Zinn.[2]

The exercise:

1. In a dignified posture, sit or lie down, or even stand up if you so desire, in a comfortable position in a space where you will not be disturbed. Turn off your phone and, if you wish, turn on some soft background music and dim the lights in the room.
2. If you lie down, you might want to do so on a soft surface such as your bed or a mat. You may use a small pillow under your head and a bolster under your knees, a folded blanket or towel beneath your lumbar area, and a rolled-up a towel or blanket under your ankles for support.
3. Gently close your eyes or, if you wish, you may keep them open. Take your mind to your nostrils and start noticing your inbreath and your outbreath.
4. Once your mind is clear and anchored in the present moment, bring to mind a photograph of when you were a small child of say four or five and imagine sitting in front of that child and looking into that child's eyes.
5. Tenderly say to that child, "May you be well, may you

be happy, may you be peaceful, may you be loved. May you be free from danger, may you enjoy mental happiness, physical happiness, and ease of well-being. I assure you that if I were to see you in need of help, I will be there to help you."

6. In your mind, imagine reaching toward that child and tenderly embracing and cuddling him or her, extending all love and compassion toward the child —
toward you.

7. Now, bring to mind a photograph of a loved one. It could be a spouse, your partner, a sibling, some other relative, or even a pet. (Not a friend, that comes next.)

8. Envision that loved one saying to you, "May you be well, may you be happy, may you be peaceful, may you be loved. May you be free from danger, may you enjoy mental happiness, physical happiness, and ease of well-being. I assure you that if I were to see you in need of help, I will be there to help you." Or, you may add any other words of love and kindness that come to you.

9. As you feel ready, and whenever you feel ready, see if you can become the source as well as the object of these same feelings. Imagine that you are responding to that loved one by looking into his or her eyes and saying, "May you be well, may you be happy, may you be peaceful, may you be loved. May you be free from danger, may you enjoy mental happiness, physical happiness, and ease of well-being. I assure you that if I were to see you in need of help, I will be there to help you." And again, you may say any other

words of compassion and tenderness that come
to you.

10. In your mind, you can envision reaching over and
hugging that loved one, extending all love and empathy
toward him or her.

11. Now, bring to mind a photograph of a friend with
whom you share intimacies, and perhaps you may
remember the last time you interacted with that friend.
Imagine looking into that friend's eyes and with feelings
of love and kindness and regard, say to that friend,
"May you be well, may you be happy, may you be
peaceful, may you be loved. May you be free from
danger, may you enjoy mental happiness, physical
happiness, and ease of well-being. I assure you that if I
were to see you in need of help, I will be there to help
you." And as you did before, use any other words of
affection and compassion that resonate with you.

12. Proceed by taking a moment to think about the last
stranger you ran into. It could be the person who
checked you out at the grocery store, a clerk at the post
office or bank, the man or woman who stopped next to
you at a traffic light or a stop sign. Just someone about
whom you know nothing. That person could be black,
gay, Hispanic, from a different country, but nonetheless
that person is another human being who more than
likely has to cope with important issues just as you do
— moments of suffering ... moments of joy.

13. And imagining with great vividness the feelings of love
and kindness and regard, say to that person, "May you

be well, may you be happy, may you be peaceful, may you be loved. May you be free from danger, may you enjoy mental happiness, physical happiness, and ease of well-being. I assure you that if I were to see you in need of help, I will be there to help you."

14. Now think of someone who is causing you difficulties. Perhaps not your worst enemy, but an adversary with whom you disagree. Someone whose behavior you do not condone. And if you have difficulty thinking of such a person, perhaps you can imagine someone treating you in that way. And even though you don't see eye to eye with the person, you know that the person is another human being who, just as you, wants to be happy. So, to that person you bequeath your loving kindness: "May you be well, may you be happy, may you be peaceful, may you be loved. May you be free from danger, may you enjoy mental happiness, physical happiness, and ease of well-being. I assure you that if I were to see you in need of help, I will be there to help you." You don't do this in hopes that the person will change — although that may happen — but I assure you, you will feel much better after doing this.

15. Proceed by thinking about all living beings on the surface of our planet, especially animals that are abused and neglected or pets that are mistreated or harmed. And as you think of these, extend to them the expressions of loving kindness: "May you be well, may you be happy, may you be peaceful, may you be loved. May you be free from danger, may you be happy. I

assure you that if I were to see you being mistreated of abused, I will be there to intervene." Just imagine a young puppy happily wagging its tail!

16. Take your mind to your nostrils and start noticing your inbreath and your outbreath, and perhaps you would like to practice a little "soft-belly" breathing.

17. Whether you have been doing this exercise lying on your back or sitting down, I invite you to let your mind go to your feet. Imagine little openings on the soles of your feet. Let your mind go to the crown of your head and imagine an opening on the crown of your head about one inch in diameter.

18. Using your imagination, envision breathing in through your feet, envisioning the breath rush up your legs, your pelvis, your torso, your neck, and when the breath gets into your head, expel it out through the imaginary opening on the crown of your head. Imagine getting rid of all the toxins in your body, breathing in fresh oxygenated air, flushing out all negativity that is within you — no need to identify it, just get rid of it.

19. And if you wish, you may reverse the direction of breathing — inhaling through the crown of your head and exhaling through the soles of your feet.

20. When you are ready, you may bring sensation back into the body by wiggling your fingers, your toes, bringing your arm overhead and stretching, and pointing and flexing your feet.

21. If you have been doing the exercise lying down on your back, to get up safely, grab the right knee with both

hands and pull it tightly into the chest, then put it down.

22. Do the same thing with the left knee.

23. Then grab both knees, bring the up towards your chest, and gently start rocking side to side.

24. Eventually rock all the way to the left, form a little pillow under your head with your left arm, and rest there for a brief moment.

25. When you are ready to get up, stretch your top leg downward. Place your right hand on the floor in front of your chest and, applying pressure with the right arm, come to a seated position.

26. Whether sitting down or lying on your back, briskly rub the palms of your hands together to generate some heat. If you wear glasses, take them off. Then cover your eyes with your hands and enjoy the warmth.

27. Take a few moments to notice how you feel and to congratulate yourself for taking the time to take care of yourself. And always remember as you bestow your loving kindness on mankind that "All Lives Can't Matter Until Black Lives Matter."

Conclusion

Loving kindness, to paraphrase Kabat-Zinn,[3] would be as if taking on these feelings of love and compassion for yourself and others, lingering, if you will, with the rhythm of your breath and your heart. This would be analogous to the all-loving embrace between a mother and her child — you embrace humanity. By practicing Metta, your own complete acceptance of yourself as you are right now allows you to let go of any feelings of being self-sustaining — rescinding any negativity, self-criticism, self-loathing, or denunciation of others that may lie beneath the surface of your psyche. You soon learn that "All Lives Can't Matter Until Black Lives Matter."

To end, I would like to finish with a poem I wrote a few years ago that shows a random act of kindness without expectation.

The Lady in the Maze[4]

*In the middle of the maze
confused and despaired,
she stands, paralyzed,
forgetting where she's been
and not knowing where to go.*

*And you,
who can traverse the maze
in the shadows of the night
knowing where you've been
and knowing where to go,
step in to offer
the gift without expectation
of journeying her
through a maze
of bewilderment and chaos.*

*And in the middle of the maze,
guiding her to mysterious places, you
carry your valise
full of bewilderment
and chaos of your own.*

11

AUTOGENICS

"'I am at peace' is understood well, the student should appreciate that this instruction is not an exercise — it is just an experience."

~ Johannes Heinrich Schultz

German psychologist Johannes Heinrich Schultz[1] developed autogenic training in 1932 as a way to have the client gain a level of control over the body. Schultz noticed that individuals undergoing hypnosis entered a relaxed state in which they experienced feelings of heaviness and warmth in their limbs. Recognizing this, he sought to recreate that state in people to reduce tension and anxiety by suggesting that the client focus on the sensation of heaviness and warmth while lying on their backs. Today, it is a type of relaxation technique that can be used to help reduce anxiety, including that experienced as part of *social anxiety disorder* (SAD).[2]

Therapists often use the technique in conjunction with cognitive-behavioral therapy (CBT). It is an intervention a client may use on their own as a self-help strategy.

Although less well-known than other relaxation techniques, e.g., progressive muscle relaxation or guided imagery, it has been used to help individuals calm down, bring the mind to the preset moment, and recognize their selflessness.

Preparing for Autogenics

1. Begin by lying down on your back, preferably on a soft surface such as your bed or a mat. You may use a small pillow under your head and a bolster under your knees, or even a folded blanket or towel beneath your lumbar area for support. You may also roll up a towel or blanket to place under your ankles for support.
2. Allow your arms to rest along the sides of your body, not touching your body with your hands, facing toward the ceiling if that's comfortable for you. Your heels should be about a foot to a foot and a half apart with the ankles rotating outwards.
3. Loosen any tight clothing and remove glasses or contacts.

The Exercise

1. Gently close your eyes or, if you wish, you may keep

them open. Take your mind to your nostrils and start noticing your inbreath and your outbreath.

2. Once your mind is settled and in the present moment, let it go to your left arm and start noticing the effect of gravity on your arm.

3. Gently and slowly repeat to yourself several times, "My arm feels heavy. It feels very heavy. I am completely calm. I can feel my hand and fingertips being pulled downwards. I know that I could lift up my arm if I wanted to, but it feels so heavy that if I tried to lift it up it up, I probably couldn't."

4. Now, quietly and slowly repeat to yourself several times, "My left arm feels warm. I can almost feel the blood rushing through my arteries and veins, warming up my left arm. It feels very warm. I am completely calm."

5. Now, let your mind go to your right arm and start noticing the effect of gravity on that arm.

6. Gently and slowly repeat to yourself several times, "My right arm feels heavy. It feels very heavy. I am completely calm. I can feel my right hand and fingertips being pulled downwards. I know that I could lift up my right arm if I wanted to, but it feels so heavy that if I tried to lift it up it up, I probably couldn't."

7. Now, quietly and slowly repeat to yourself several times, "My right arm feels warm. I can almost feel the blood rushing through the arteries and veins of my right arm, warming it up. It feels very warm. I am completely calm."

8. Proceed to your left leg and start noticing the effect of gravity on that leg.

9. Gently and slowly repeat to yourself several times, "My left leg feels heavy. It feels very heavy. I am completely calm. I can feel my left foot being pulled downwards and outwards. I know that I could lift up my leg if I wanted to, but it feels so heavy that if I tried to lift it up it up, I probably couldn't."

10. Now, quietly and slowly repeat to yourself several times, "My left leg feels warm. I can almost feel the blood rushing through my arteries and veins, warming up my left leg. It feels very warm. I am completely calm."

11. Continue by letting your mind go to your right leg and start noticing the effect of gravity on that leg.

12. Tenderly and slowly repeat to yourself several times, "My right leg feels heavy. It feels very heavy. I am completely calm. I can feel my right leg and foot being pulled downwards and outwards. I know that I could lift up my right leg if I wanted to, but it feels so heavy that if I tried to lift it up it up, I probably couldn't."

13. Now let your mind go to your solar plexus, the pit of your stomach. It's that spot in our bodies where a lot of tension accumulates — where we get the so-called butterflies. You may notice that it's calm. Gently and slowly repeat to yourself several times, "My solar plexus feels calm. It is quiet. My abdomen feels warm. I am completely calm."

14. At this time, let your mind go to the center of your chest. Notice that your heart is beating slowly and

rhythmically. Quietly and slowly repeat to yourself six times, "My heartbeat is calm and regular. I am completely calm."

15. Quietly and slowly let your mind go to your forehead. Repeat to yourself several times, "My forehead is pleasantly cool and relaxed. I am totally calm." Imagine strands of soft noodles lying across your forehead.

16. Finally, let your mind go to your breath and notice that your body has been breathing all along. You've had to do nothing. The body simply breathes. Repeat to yourself several times, "Breathing in, I know that I'm breathing in. Breathing out, I know I'm breathing out." Do this for several minutes.

17. I invite you to let your mind go to your feet. Imagine little openings on the soles of your feet. Let your mind go to the crown of your head and imagine an opening on the crown of your head about one inch in diameter.

18. Using your imagination, envision breathing in through your feet, envision the breath rush up your legs, your pelvis, your torso, your neck, and when the breath gets into your head, expel it out through the imaginary opening on the crown of your head. Imagine getting rid of all the toxins in your body, breathing in fresh oxygenated air, flushing out all negativity that is within you — no need to identify it, just get rid of it.

19. And if you wish, you may reverse the direction of breathing — inhaling through the crown of your head and exhaling through the soles of your feet.

20. When you are ready, you may bring sensation back into

the body by wiggling your fingers, your toes, bringing your arm overhead and stretching, and pointing and flexing your feet.

21. To get up safely, grab the right knee with both hands and pull it tightly into the chest, then put it down.

22. Do the same thing with the left knee.

23. Then grab both knees, bring them up to your chest, and gently start rocking side to side.

24. Eventually rock all the way to the left, form a little pillow under your head with your left arm, and rest there for a brief moment.

25. When you are ready to get up, stretch your top leg downward. Place your right hand on the floor in from of your chest and, applying pressure with the right arm, come to a seated position.

26. Now briskly rub the palms of your hands together to generate some heat. If you wear glasses, take them off. Then cover your eyes with your hands and enjoy the warmth.

27. Take a few moments to notice how you feel and to congratulate yourself for taking the time to take care of yourself.

Conclusion

Again, this is an exercise you can do on your own to relax, calm down, bring the mind to the present moment, and recognize your selflessness.

Or you may simply do a random act of loving kindness:

- Call a friend that you haven't spoken with in a while.
- Send a few dollars to someone you know who's in need in an envelope without a return address.
- Send a letter to a grandparent or another loved one.
- Send flowers to a friend.
- Tell someone you love them.
- Offer to pick up some groceries for your elderly neighbor.
- Send someone a handwritten note.
- Pay for a meal for someone in need.
- Mow a disabled neighbor's lawn.
- Offer to babysit for a friend.
- Walk your friend's dog.
- Remember that "All Lives Can't Matter Until Black Lives Matter."

12

WALKING MEDITATION

"But the beauty is in the walking — we are betrayed by destinations."

~ Gwyn Thomas

*T*urn a ten-minute walk into an everyday activity for mindfulness, stress reduction, calming down, recognizing our selflessness, and promoting racial justice.

This kind of meditation is not about getting somewhere by walking. Instead, you are noticing each step, being fully there, wherever you actually are. You are not trying to get anywhere — there is no arriving other than continually getting to wherever you are in the present moment.

Walking meditation can be practiced at any speed. We can go from slow, mindful walking to fast, mindful running. But to begin formal mindful walking, it is best to start very slowly, to tune down the instinct of walking fast, as well as to refine our awareness with the sensations associated with walking, the breath, and what is going on in the mind.

As you walk, pay close attention to the movements of your body — the swinging of your arms, the lifting of your legs and landing of your feet on the warm pavement, the tree branches on the sidewalk etched by the light of a blazing sun, the perspiration on your skin, the rubbing of your clothing against your bronzed flesh. And now and then you glance at the scenery around you and you are there, wherever you are. It may be you've opted to take this mindful walk outdoors on a foggy day and you feel the mist caress your skin. Or in the late evening, when the moon is intrepid enough to show its presence next to a nearby, roaming Jupiter.

And you become aware that you are part of the universe, that you are a member of the tribe — just enjoying the journey with no intention of getting anywhere, one foot, one step at a time. There is no disembarking at any port other than continually landing in the present moment.

The Moon and Jupiter[1]
Can you see Jupiter
indefatigably chasing
a bright crescent moon on
that passive, cloudless
cerulean sky?

So near to each other
they seem.

So serene!

It's as if they were roving together in
a palliative realm
of euphoric nothingness.

A fulfilled
destinationless pilgrimage…

To places unknown.

With walking, we can enjoy our bodies differently than by sitting or lying down. We are not static. We are moving, feeling our body shift from one position to the next, noticing our breath and taking in all that is going on around us, watching our mind, not allowing it to leave us so we can enjoy the vividness and exquisiteness available to us right now.

How to Do It

This is a ten-minute walking meditation exercise.[2]

Before you begin your meditation, find a quiet space to walk. It could be outdoors, or in a hallway, or even a large room, walking back and forth.

1. **Begin to walk at an extremely slow pace.** Place your hands wherever they are comfortable: on your belly, behind your back, or let your arms hang down at your sides.

- If useful, you may count your steps up to ten. Then start back at one and continue. If you're in a small room, as you reach ten, intentionally pause for a moment and then turn around and proceed with your walking.
- With each step, notice the lifting and falling of each foot. Notice how your legs and the rest of your body moves, especially the side to side movements.
- Become aware of anything else that captures your attention, especially your breathing. Notice that your mind will drift, so gently but firmly bring it back again and again to the present moment.
- If you are doing this outdoors, be aware of the scenery around you, taking it all in.

2. **Now for a few minutes, pay attention to sounds around you.** Whether you're indoors, in the woods, or in a city, pay attention to the sounds. Don't try to label anything; just simply listen.

3. **Shift your attention to your sense of smell.** Again, simply notice. Don't try to label anything; just simply smell.

4. **Now, allow your attention to shift to your vision,** colors and objects and whatever else you see, gently but firmly bringing the mind to your walking if it has drifted. Always try to remain open to what you're seeing, not overreacting or daydreaming but just simply observing.

5. **Be aware of everything around you**, wherever you are. You have nothing to do. You are not trying to get anywhere. You are simply walking.

6. **Finally, bring your awareness back the physical sensations** of walking, noticing your feet touching the ground, the movements of your body, and your breath with each step.

7. When you're ready to end your walking meditation, stand still for a moment. Pause. Take a brief moment to end your practice and congratulate yourself for having taken the time to take care of yourself.

Conclusion

Consider the benefits of the walking meditation: you become aware of your selflessness, you recognize you're a member of the human tribe, you sense your commitment to racial justice, you know that you have trained your mind and changed the structure and function of your brain for the better, and you know that "All Lives Can't Matter Until Black Lives Matter."

To end this chapter, I would like to quote a poem I wrote a while back that shows how much we miss when we walk mindlessly.

Too Busy for Nonsense
Heavens splashed
with multicolored hues
by daybreak's sun rays.

Discordant shadows and furrows

on the sidewalk
sketched by the light
of a blooming moon.

Wind, making its presence known in
the filigreed branches
of the tree broadcasting
the arrival of a looming storm.

Early spring hills draped
with quilts of burgeoning wildflowers.

Imposing bucolic mountains contoured
by waves
of canyons and gorges.

A child's irrepressible smile
at the sight of
a nurturing mother's face.

Dissonant chirping
of early-morning,
begging hatchlings.

Tintinnabulation
of church bells
infringing on the silence
of daybreak.

You might be interested
in savoring the thrill and
mystery of these...

Yet again,
you might be too busy for
such nonsense.

13

BODY AWARENESS

"Body awareness not only anchors you in the present moment, it is a doorway out of the prison that is the ego. It also strengthens the immune system and the body's ability to heal itself."

~ Eckhart Tolle

*I*mproving an awareness of your body is an approach that is known to be a key element or a mechanism of action used to enhance well-being.

Those who have reported to have benefited from practicing body awareness, or the body scan, include clients suffering from a variety of medical conditions including chronic low back pain, pelvic pain, fibromyalgia, musculoskeletal pain, chronic pain in general, disordered eating and obesity, irritable bowel syndrome, sexual abuse trauma, coronary artery disease, congestive heart failure, chronic renal failure, falls in the elderly, anxiety, and depression.

Our purpose is to show that body awareness allows you to let go of self-centeredness and recognize that you are an integral member of the human tribe — no different from anyone else.

This intervention has proven to be an enormously powerful and healing form of meditation. It forms the core of the lying-down practices for those who train in Mindfulness-Based Stress Reduction (MBSR).

It involves the systematic scanning of the body with the mind, bringing a compassionate yet sincere and openhearted interest in the various regions of the body.

First Body Scan

When we practice the body scan, we are analytically and on purpose allowing our minds to move through our body. We pay attention to the various sensations, if any, experienced in the areas we are scanning. That we can do this at all is quite remarkable. That we can do it with intent, either spontaneously or in an orderly way, is even more so. Without moving a muscle, we can let our minds go to any part of our bodies and mindfully notice any sensation or lack thereof in that moment.

These instructions are a modification of the ones described by Jon Kabat-Zinn in *Coming to Our Senses.*[1]

1. Begin by lying down on your back, preferably on a soft surface such as your bed or a mat. You may use a small

pillow under your head and a bolster under your knees, or even a folded blanket or towel beneath your lumbar area for support. You may also roll up a towel or blanket to place under your ankles. Turn off your phone so you won't be interrupted and, if you wish, you may light a scented candle, turn on some soft background music, and dim the lights in the room.

2. Rest your arms along the side of your body, not touching the body, palms up preferably if that is comfortable for you. Your heels should be two feet to two and a half feet apart with the ankles rotating comfortably outwards.

3. Begin by taking your mind to your nostrils and proceed with a minute or so of "soft-belly" breathing to bring the mind to the present moment.

Be mindful! Always be mindful of any sensation or lack thereof you are experiencing in the part of the body you are scanning. Remember, don't chastise yourself if you feel nothing. That's perfectly normal — what you feel is <u>nothing</u>! Also, be mindful of any emotions that crop up as you scan certain areas of the body.

Caveats: If at any time you find that your body drifts into the past or into the future, gently but firmly bring it to the present moment.

Also, there may be a tendency to get sleepy. If that is the case for you, try as best you can to "fall awake." To do this, you may open your eyes and look at the ceiling for a moment or so or hold your breath for a few moments to see if that helps you stay awake.

Additionally, if there is any temptation to move while you are doing the exercise, remember you have two options — to move or not to move. As best you can, resist the temptation to move because once you start moving, you will continue to do so. If you simply have to move, say to scratch an area of the body, do so very mindfully and slowly, and as quickly as you can, return to your resting position.

And always let gravity be your friend. Just let go.

4. Once your mind is settled and in the present moment, begin by letting your mind go to your mouth and notice the contact that your tongue makes with your palate or your teeth, the amount of saliva in your mouth. Is it dry or moist. How about your lips? Are they dry … moist? Is there an impulse to moisten them with your tongue?
5. Proceed by taking your mind to your ears. What do you hear? Is it the sound of the music playing in the background if you've turned on some music? Any other sounds in the room, outside the room?
6. Now, proceed to the toes of the left foot. Move through the entire foot, including the sole, the spaces in between the toes, the heel, the top of the foot, and the ankle.

Imagine your foot being pulled downward and outward by gravity.

When you're ready, on your next inhale, direct it to the left foot; imagine it inflating, and on the outbreath, let it go. Let it dissolve.

7. Then go up the left leg, the shin, the calf, the knee, the kneecap, the thigh, the groin, and the left hip. As always, be mindful of any sensation you feel in your left leg.
   And again, as you did before, direct your next inbreath to the left leg; imagine it inflating, and on the outbreath, let it go. Let it dissolve.
8. Then switch to the toes of the right foot, the other regions of the foot, then up the right leg as you did with the left. Again, breathe into the left foot; inflate it, and on the outbreath, let it go. Let it disappear.
9. From there, the focus moves, sequentially and slowly, over the entirety of the pelvic region, including the hips again, the buttocks, the anal sphincter, and the genitals.
10. The mind proceeds to the lower back, an area of the body that gives some of us problems. If that is the case for you, notice it, breath into it, and with the outbreath, let it go.
11. Then to the upper back. Notice the shoulder blades floating in back, all the way up to the collarbone and shoulders.
12. Go to the abdomen — your belly. Feel it inflate and deflate as you breathe in and you breathe out.

13. Go to the upper torso, the rib cage, the breasts, and nipples.

14. Become aware of the heart beating and lungs breathing, as well as the great vessels housed within the rib cage.

15. From the shoulders, move to both arms, starting from the tips of the fingers and thumbs and moving successively through the fingers, the palms, and backs of the hands, the wrists, forearms, elbows, upper arms, armpits, and shoulders again.

    Become aware of the knuckles, fingernails, and all the blood vessels and nerves that crisscross the hands. Perhaps you'd like to think of a small task you did earlier in the day such as brushing your teeth or using a fork to feed yourself. Think of the mystery and miracle of those hands!

16. Then move into the area of the neck and throat. Become aware of the larynx or your voice box. Take a moment to think about when you're dialoguing with another person. Are you listening to prepare yourself to respond or are you listening to learn something from the other person … to learn how you may be able to alleviate some of their suffering?

17. Finally, proceed to the face and head. Notice your brow. Imagine strands of soft noodles lying across your brow. Envision your eyeballs gently sinking into your eye sockets and your cheeks being pulled down by gravity.

18. Now, I invite you to let your mind go to your feet. Imagine little openings on the soles of your feet. Let your mind go to the crown of your head and imagine

an opening on the crown of your head about one inch in diameter.

19. Using your imagination, envision breathing in through your feet, envision the breath rush up your legs, your pelvis, your torso, your neck, and when the breath gets into your head, expel it out through the imaginary opening on the crown of your head. Imagine getting rid of all the toxins in your body, breathing in fresh oxygenated air, flushing out all negativity that is within you — no need to identify it, just get rid of it.

20. And if you wish, you may reverse the direction of breathing — inhaling through the crown of your head and exhaling through the soles of your feet.

21. When you are ready, you may bring sensation back into the body by wiggling your fingers, your toes, bringing your arm overhead and stretching, and pointing and flexing your feet.

22. To get up safely, grab the right knee with both hands and pull it tightly into the chest, then put it down.

23. Do the same thing with the left knee.

24. Then grab both knees, bring them up to the chest, and gently start rocking side to side.

25. Eventually rock all the way to the left, form a little pillow under your head with your left arm, and rest there for a brief moment.

26. When you are ready to get up, stretch your top leg downward. Place your right hand on the floor in front of your chest and, applying pressure with the right arm, come to a seated position.

27. Now briskly rub the palms of your hands together to generate some heat. If you wear glasses, take them off. Then cover your eyes with your hands and enjoy the warmth.

28. Take a few moments to notice how you feel and to congratulate yourself for taking the time to take care of yourself.

Second Body Scan

This second version of the body scan is a modification of the one described by James Gordon in his book *The Transformation*.[2] As with any mindfulness intervention, there is no right or wrong way to do it. As Dr. Kabat-Zinn used to tell me when I was training under him, "Just do it!"

You may sit or lie down for this exercise or, if you wish, stand. Dr. Gordon suggests some soft music in the background. It will ease your progress through the exercise and help the body and organs yield their wisdom. I personally recommend lying down for this exercise.

You may want to start by getting a bird's-eye view of the body's major systems — cardiovascular, digestive, musculoskeletal, etc. You can find these in Netter's *Atlas of the Human Anatomy*[3] or just spend a little time searching for human anatomy images on the internet.

1. Begin by lying down on your back, preferably on a soft surface such as your bed or a mat. You may use a small pillow under your head and a bolster under your knees,

or even a folded blanket or towel beneath your lumbar area for support. You may also roll up a towel or blanket to place under your ankles. Turn off your phone so you won't be interrupted and, if you wish, you may light a scented candle, turn on some soft background music, and dim the lights in the room.

2. Rest your arms along the side of your body, not touching the body, palms up preferably if that is comfortable for you. Your heels should be two feet to two and a half feet apart with the ankles rotating comfortably outwards.

3. Begin by taking your mind to your nostrils and proceed with a minute or so of "soft-belly" breathing to bring the mind to the present moment.

Be mindful! Always be mindful of any sensation or lack thereof you are experiencing in the part of the body you are scanning. Remember, don't chastise yourself if you feel nothing. That's perfectly normal — what you feel is nothing! Also, be mindful of any emotions that crop up as you scan certain areas of the body.

Caveats: If at any time you find that your body drifts into the past or into the future, gently but firmly bring it to the present moment.

Also, there may be a tendency to get sleepy. If that is the case for you, try as best you can to "fall awake." To do this, you may open your eyes and look at the ceiling for a moment or so or hold your breath for a few moments to see if that helps you stay awake.

Additionally, if there is any temptation to move while you are doing the exercise, remember you have two options—to move or not to move. As best you can, resist the temptation to move because once you start moving, you will continue to do so. If you simply have to move, say to scratch an area of the body, do so very mindfully and slowly, and as quickly as you can, return to your resting position.
Always let gravity be your friend. Just let go.

4. Begin with the "soft-belly" breathing in through your nose and out through your mouth until your mind is settled in the present moment.

5. In your mind, follow your breath into your lungs and move with it as it flows with your blood through your body.

6. Proceed to your heart. Imagine yourself sitting in your heart. Perhaps there is a sense of pain, curiosity, or wonder. Feel and listen. Ask yourself, "Why am I being called here?" And perhaps, "Why is my heart giving me trouble? What do I need to learn?" Simply ask questions and wait for answers. "How can what I am feeling in my heart give me an answer?"

7. Now, feel yourself moving with your blood as it leaves your heart and moves up into your shoulders and then down into your arms and hands and fingers. Perhaps, as

you did with the previous scan, you'd like to wonder about the mystery and miracle of your hands.

8. Return slowly and gently to your heart and become aware of yourself there.

9. Now move with your blood and your breath up through your aorta and then as it curves down through your chest, past your diaphragm, which separates your chest from your abdomen, and into your belly. What is my belly telling me? Do you feel any gurgling (borborygmus)? Am I eating too much ... the wrong kind of diet?

10. Imagining all of the organs in your body, become aware of blood flowing through your stomach and onto the spleen on your left then to your liver, pancreas, and gallbladder on your right.

11. At this time, become aware of the blood flowing farther down, nourishing your small intestine, then your large intestine, continuing through to your rectum and anus. Notice once more the blood flowing down the middle of your body, this time out to your kidneys through your pelvis and into your bladder.
    If you're a woman, feel the blood and its life-giving oxygen bringing you to your ovaries, your uterus, and your vagina. If organs have been removed or altered in any way, become aware of the structures that are present and of what is missing.
    If you're a man, feel yourself moving with your breath and blood into your prostate, penis, and testes.

12. Allow your consciousness to extend your journey,

moving with your breath and your blood down into your thighs and your calves, your feet and your toes.

13. Allow the sound of the music to bring you back to your heart, becoming aware of yourself once again resting within your heart. Become aware of its beating. Stay there for a few moments.

14. Continue by letting the sound of the music take you to a place in your body that's calling out to you. It may be a place where you have chronic pain. It may be an organ that once gave you problems or one that you're curious about. It may be a place that, surprisingly, attracts you in this moment.

15. Simply move with the sound of the music and the oxygen moving in your blood. Your awareness is moving and that place in your body is calling to you, saying, "Come here. Come now."

16. Once there, look around. What it's like to be there? What does it look like, feel like, sound like, or smell like? Are you comfortable being there? "What am I doing here?" "Why was I called here?" "What do you have to tell me?" Each time you ask a question, wait for the answer. And when the answer comes, continue asking. Perhaps it's telling you, "You need to take better care of me. You must help me. I'm hurting." It could be your liver, your kidneys, your right or left lung. Perhaps you've been having feelings of superiority, drinking too much, or eating too many fatty foods.

17. Then you may want to ask yourself, "What should I do?" And the first answer may be amazingly simple.

"I'm going to work on becoming less self-centered and less discriminating against others, cut down on my drinking, or stop eating so many fatty foods."

18. Now, remember this is all in your mind. Your anger may still be there, but you may be too afraid to express it. You may be acting like everything's okay, but deep inside perhaps you're suffering too much. Perhaps you've been discriminating against Black people, gays, or Hispanics; drinking too much to drown your anger; or not watching your diet. It might help to write your emotions down in a journal or pound your anger out on a pillow. You may need to leave the relationship you're in. "Well, perhaps I should tell my partner that I'm angry because he throws his clothes all over the house and doesn't clean up after himself."

19. Continue the dialogue, asking whatever you need to ask, paying close attention to the answers. And after you feel satisfied with the answers, thank your liver, your heart, your kidneys, any organ you can think of, thank your body, which is so clever, for helping you.

20. Continue letting the sound of the music and the flow of blood and the oxygen moving through your veins bring you back to your heart. Relax here for a few moments, being aware of yourself, breathing, relaxing, feeling the warmth and strength, the life-giving spirit of your breath and your heartbeat.

21. If you wish, you may continue letting the sound of the music and the flow of blood take you to another part of your body — say your tailbone, your sacrum, or your

buttock — and keep on going with the exercise to other parts of your body.

22. When you're ready to finish, I invite you to let your mind go to your feet. Imagine little openings on the soles of your feet. Let your mind go to the crown of your head and imagine an opening on the crown of your head about one inch in diameter.

23. Using your imagination, envision breathing in through your feet, envision the breath rush up your legs, your pelvis, your torso, your neck, and when the breath gets into your head, expel it out through the imaginary opening on the crown of your head. Imagine getting rid of all the toxins in your body, breathing in fresh oxygenated air, flushing out all negativity that is within you — no need to identify it, just get rid of it.

24. And if you care to, you may reverse the direction of breathing — inhaling through the crown of your head and exhaling through the soles of your feet.

25. Now, bring sensation back into the body by wiggling your fingers, your toes, bringing your arm overhead and stretching, and pointing and flexing your feet.

26. To get up safely, grab the right knee with both hands and pull it tightly into the chest, then put it down.

27. Do the same thing with the left knee.

28. Then grab both knees, bring them up to your chest, and gently start rocking side to side.

29. In due time, rock all the way to the left, form a little pillow under your head with your left arm, and rest there for a brief moment.

30. To get up, stretch your top leg downward. Place your right hand on the floor in front of your chest and, applying pressure with the right arm, come to a seated position.

31. Briskly rub the palms of your hands together to generate some heat. If you wear glasses, take them off. Then cover your eyes with your hands and enjoy the warmth.

32. Notice how you feel at this very moment and congratulate yourself for taking the time to take care of yourself.

Conclusion

The best way to unwind is to stop trying to make things different from what they are. Simply allow whatever is going on to go on rather than attempting to create something else.

Accepting things the way they are in the present moment is the way to relate and respond rather than react to experiences that hook us.

For example, if you notice that your mind is in the so-called default mode, the daydreaming mode, stop and become fully aware of the four fundamentals of mindfulness — your breath, your body, your mind, and the impermanence of all phenomena in life.

By allowing yourself to notice where your physical sensations are strongest, you'll be able to focus on the now. And since the breath is always with you, you may always allude to the "soft-belly" breathing technique discussed earlier.

Once you have become aware of the sensations in the different parts of your body or organs, you may say to yourself, "I'm okay. Whatever is going on at this moment is okay. It's okay to feel the way I feel under these circumstances."

Just establish a relationship with your breath and your body, remembering that, as Jon Kabat-Zinn said, *"As long as you are breathing, there is more right with you than there is wrong, no matter what is wrong."*

Acceptance is not giving up. Acceptance is an essential mechanism to recognizing the vicissitudes of life and how to respond appropriately to the difficulties and obstacles that arise in our lives rather than reacting automatically in an out-of-control manner.

14

SITTING MEDITATION

"You do not need to leave your room. Remain sitting at your table and listen. Do not even listen, simply wait, be quiet, still and solitary. The world will freely offer itself to you to be unmasked, it has no choice, it will roll in ecstasy at your feet."

~ Franz Kafka

Sitting meditation isn't one-size-fits-all; a plethora of variations and techniques are available to the meditator.

Simply sit back, relax, breathe, pay attention to your body, notice what your mind is saying to you, and watch the moment evolve from moment to moment.

Sitting meditation can be done anytime, anywhere, and for any length of time. Whether you're exploring it for the first time or are a seasoned meditator, it is important to be *comfortable* as you sit. Just adjust your practice to fit your lifestyle, work schedule, and needs.

Sitting in a Chair

If you opt to sit in a chair, get in the right position to meditate. Sit with a straight back and your feet flat on the floor. Your upper and lower legs should be at a ninety-degree angle with your knees. You may need to slide to the edge of the chair to get into the right position. Sit so that your head and neck are in line with your spine.

Kneeling Down in a Japanese Style Position

If you are in a place where you can comfortably kneel down, you may want to do so. The advantage to this is that it will keep your spine straight. The disadvantage is that this places great strain on the knees, causing the patellar ligaments and tendons in the knee joints to stretch or even tear.

Lotus Position

If your hips are flexible, you may sit in quarter, half, or full lotus position. You may also sit cross-legged with your hips elevated higher than your heels. For this, you may use a meditation cushion (a zafu), a folded towel, or a pillow. You may also use a meditation bench, which helps support and keep the spine straight.

The Spine

No matter how you sit, your spine should be as straight as possible. If you slouch forward or sway slightly backward, gently but firmly remind yourself to correct your posture.

The Hands

You may cup your hands on your belly in the Cosmic Mudra (a hand gesture used in Hindu and Buddhist practices). This hand posture is commonly used in zazen, a form of sitting meditation practiced by Zen Buddhists. To adopt this mudra, allow your dominant hand to cradle the other hand, with both palms facing up. The tips of your thumbs should be touching each other, forming a compressed oval shape together with your palms. This mudra is said to generate more heat and energy.

You also may rest your hands on your thighs, palms facing up or down. That is said to be more grounding and helps relax your body's energy flow.

The Chin Mudra is another hand posture you may use. It connects us to our higher Self, helps lift dull energy, creates a more receptive state, calms the mind, and brightens the overall mood. For this posture, rest your hands on your thighs. Gently tuck the tip of the index finger under the tip of the thumb, keeping the remaining three fingers lightly extended downward. Place your hands on your thighs with the palms facing upward.

Shoulders

Your shoulders should be relaxed and comfortable, drawn slightly back and down away from your ears. Notice if one shoulder is higher than the other. This helps keep your heart center open and your back straight.

Chin, Neck, and Jaw

Your chin should be slightly tucked while maintaining length in the back of your neck and spine. By positioning your chin and neck appropriately, you'll be able to maintain your posture. Relax to release any tension in the face. Also, allow the jaw to relax.

Eyes

You may wish to meditate with your eyes closed, as most meditators do. However, some people like to meditate with their eyes open, gazing downwards toward the floor, keeping their face relaxed and avoiding squinting.

Be Comfortable

It is particularly important to choose a position that is comfortable for you. Otherwise you will not be able to focus on your meditation.

Things to Remember

- Start with short practices and increase as you become a more seasoned meditator.
- Concentrate on your breath, noticing the expansion and contraction of the abdomen and/or torso with the inhale and exhale — the "soft-belly" breathing.
- Breathe slowly, deeply, and smoothly.
- Be mindful of the thoughts, feelings, and sensations that you experience from moment to moment without

any judgment. Remember that these can be positive, negative, neutral, pleasant, unpleasant, from the past, the present, or projecting into the future.

- Gently bring your mind back to the present without judgment when it wanders.
- Be conscious of the silence and stillness within.
- Bring your awareness to the sounds around you one by one.
- Feel the air or clothing touching your skin and feel your body touching the floor.
- During your practice, check in with your posture from time to time to ensure that your spine is straight and your shoulders are down and away from your ears.

The Practice Mindfulness of Sounds and Thoughts

This exercise is a sitting meditation that focuses on sounds heard and thoughts that go through the mind as one sits quietly.

1. Practice mindfulness of breath and body, as described earlier, until you feel reasonably settled. That is, the "soft-belly" breath.
2. Sit as instructed above.
3. Concentrate on your awareness to shift from sensations in the body to hearing. Bring your attention to the ears, and then allow the awareness to open and expand, so that there is a receptiveness to sounds as they arise, wherever they arise.
4. There is no need to go searching for sounds or listening for particular sounds. Instead, as best you can, simply

open your mind so that it is receptive to awareness of sounds from all directions as they arise — sounds that are close, sounds that are far away, sounds that are in front, behind, to the side, above or below. Open to a whole space of sound around you. Be aware of obvious sounds and of more subtle sounds, aware of the space between sounds, aware of silence.

5. As best you can, be aware of sounds simply as sensations. When you find that you are thinking about the sounds, reconnect, as best you can, with direct awareness of their sensory qualities (patterns of pitch, timbre, loudness, and duration), rather than their meanings or implications.

6. As always, whenever you notice that your awareness is no longer focused on sounds in the moment, gently acknowledge where the mind has moved to, and then retune the awareness back to sounds as they arise and pass from one moment to the next.

7. Imagine now that your right ear is plugged up and all sounds are coming in through the left ear. Notice your ability to do this. Continue doing this for a few minutes.

8. Next, switch. Imagine the left ear plugged up, letting all the sounds come in through the right ear. Amazing, eh?

9. Mindfulness of sound can be an unbelievably helpful practice on its own as a way of expanding mindfulness and giving it a more open, spacious quality, whether or not the practice is preceded by awareness of sensations or followed, as here, by awareness of thoughts.

10. Proceed by letting go of awareness of sounds and refocus your attention on what's going on in your mind. Just as with focusing on sounds, notice the thoughts as they arise, develop, and disappear. No need to try to make thoughts come or go. Just let them arise naturally as you did with the sounds, letting them come and go at will.

11. Some meditators find it helpful to bring awareness to thoughts in the mind as if they were being projected on a screen at the movies. You sit, looking at the screen, waiting for the thoughts to show up on the screen. You watch it until the thought disappears, then let it go.

12. To finish the exercise, briskly rub the palms of your hands together to generate some heat. If you wear glasses, take them off. Then cover your eyes with your warm hands and enjoy.

13. Take a few moments to notice how you feel and to congratulate yourself for taking the time to take care of yourself.

Conclusion

As with any other meditation, taking time to sit for a few moments and simply listen to the sounds around you while you pay attention to your breath, the sensations in your body, and the thoughts that cross your mind will provide you with all of the benefits of mindfulness discussed in Chapter 4.

And as you become a more seasoned meditator, you will become more selfless, more grounded, and more in touch with who you are as a human being and how you fit into the mosaic that makes up the human tribe. For that matter, you'll be able to savor the fact that you have been invited to spend some time living on this planet, even it is just but for what is in the realm of an imperceptible moment.

To finish this chapter, I would like to cite a small poem I wrote a few years ago.

As You See It[1]

The world is, as
you see it.

As you see it, the
world is not.

The world is, as
it is.
What is,
you may not see.

15

SHAKING AND SWAYING

One way to let go and release energy from the body and mind is to shake and sway as described by James Gordon.[1] The technique loosens the tendency to fight or flee (the fight/flight response) and allows you to become selfless — get rid of any anger and feeling of superiority or inferiority that you may be holding on to.

Technically it is a form of "expressive" or *attentive* meditation, perhaps the oldest form of meditation known to man. The other two are *constructive* and *destructive*.[2]

If you're willing to try it, let's begin.

1. Settle down with some "soft-belly" breathing.
2. After you've settled down, put on some fast music (Dr. Gordon suggests Osho's "Dynamic Meditation") and just let your body move and shake to it. I don't mean

"dance" or you'll say to yourself, "I never really learned how to dance." This is not about dancing; it's about moving and shaking your body.

3. Put your feet about shoulder-width apart, bending your knees a little bit. Relax your body and start shaking. Always start from your feet, up through your knees, then your hips, to your belly, up your rib cage, then your shoulder, neck, and head until your whole body is shaking. Let the shaking take control.

4. Do so for about six minutes.

5. No matter how ridiculous you look, close your eyes if you care to and just shake as fast as you can. Laugh! Shout! Keep on shaking. Do it and see how incredibly well you'll feel.

6. When the six minutes are over, stop. Take a few "soft-belly" breaths and say to yourself, "Thank you, Nature, for this experience"!

7. Now begin rocking and swaying to softer, slower music you might enjoy — perhaps Beethoven's "Moonlight Sonata" or "African Dream Lounge."

8. Again, begin rocking and swaying, starting from your feet up through your knees, hips, and shoulders to your chest, until your entire body is rocking and swaying. Let the music be your guide. Let go of your shoulders — so much tension accumulates there. KEEP GOING. Let the rocking and swaying take over your whole body. Good!

9. Keep on laughing, enjoying, and when the six minutes

are over, STOP. Be still, and take a few "soft-belly" breaths.

10. Finally, you feel relaxed. You can feel your body again. What happened to the tension, anger, and sense of superiority I had in me? Why was I overwhelmed by so much tragedy?

Always remember that the movements always go from the feet up through the knees to the hips, the belly, the rib cage, and the shoulders, neck, and head until the entire body is moving.

Conclusion

The benefits of expressive (or attentive) meditations such as this one include boosts in the feel-good neurotransmitters, serotonin, dopamine, and the endorphins. They also include creation of new neurons in the hippocampus, as well as decreased anxiety, greater resilience, better mood, relief against depression, improved sleep and sharpened memory, and greater capacity to focus.

It is highly likely that shaking and swaying and the other styles of expressive meditations, when done regularly, will impact your life and make you recognize that —

"All Lives Can't Matter Until Black Lives Matter."

EPILOGUE

"But maybe if I show up every day as a human, a good human, doing wonderful things, loving my family, loving your kids, taking care of things that I care about — maybe, just maybe that work will pick away at the scabs of your discrimination."

~ Michelle Obama

The year was 1961. Until then, I had lived in the Caribbean, on the Island of Puerto Rico, where I was born, and in Europe. That year, I went to Augusta, Georgia, to continue my undergraduate education at the Medical College of Georgia. To my dismay, I encountered the "Whites Only" and "Colored Only" signs everywhere I turned.

This included the hospital where I went to work as a laboratory technician, the University Hospital, which had two wings — the

Lamar wing for "the colored" and the Jennings wing for the "whites."

My first task was to go for a blood draw. To my surprise, there were two blood-drawing trays with the appropriate syringes and test tubes for the collection of human blood samples. One marked "Lamar" (named after Gazeway B. Lamar, who had left funds from his estate "for the building of two hospitals for the exclusive care of 'Negro patients'") and the other "Jennings" (named after Dr. Will Jennings, an Augusta, Georgia surgeon and two times mayor of the city).

Not knowing which tray to use, I asked the supervisor of the day to explain. Her sincere, matter-of-fact explanation was bewildering to me. Why go to the trouble of having two blood-drawing trays when a vein is a vein, and red blood is red blood?

After a brief parse into the history of this new country I was calling home, I learned that ever since enslaved Black people arrived on the shores of the English colony of Virginia in 1619, white legislators at various levels of government had designed laws to explicitly control and suppress Black lives — something that apparently was still going on.

Along with my deracination of the historical backdrop, I also learned, by eavesdropping, that I was the token Puerto Rican at the hospital. Little did I know that had I been around in the early 1900s, President Wilson, on March 2, 1917, under the Jones-Shafroth Act, would have granted me statutory American social responsibility. A great convenience for a country that needed manpower, a cabalistic way of referring to peonage for its Armed Forces at that time.

Not wanting to stir up too much furor, I proceed to the "Whites Only" Jennings wing to draw red blood samples from Caucasian veins, then to the Blacks only wing to draw equally red blood samples from Black lives at the "Colored Only" Lamar wing.

A few weeks thereafter I went to the Miller Theater in downtown Augusta to see a movie and wanted to go to sit in the balcony, where I preferred to sit, and there it was: "Colored Only." Apparently, the balcony of theaters was reserved for Black lives by white legislators of Georgia.

And when traveling along Interstate 20 for the first time to go to Atlanta for a meeting at the CDC, nature called and I had to stop at a rest stop and encountered two rest rooms and two water fountains, those for "Whites Only" and for "Colored Only."

Yes, this was the America I had come to in 1961.

Countless people with good intentions quietly know that discrimination is still alive and doing well in the United States. They see how campaign rallies equate to Roman venues displaying the horrors of bloodshed and carnage.

Despite the fact that our national anthem dictates that we live in "the home of the free," we live in a country where attacking people who are different is a deplorable display of unacceptable legerdemain. Politicians are saying, and continue to say, seditious atrocities that deserve "spanking."

Nevertheless, I believe that deep inside, mankind understands our egalitarian nature, that there is no such thing as *race*, that, again, we all descend from the same maternal womb, that we were born to be happy, make others happy, and alleviate the suffering of those who suffer.

As I have said before, we are born with innate goodness. But on the other hand, silence and tumult are understandable. We need to educate ourselves and be mindful, speak out, and shout out our opprobrium for racism. Our leaders at an international level must communicate with each other and make it clear to the world that:

" All Lives Can't Matter Until Black Lives Matter."

APPENDIX 1
THE PROTESTS

On May 25, 2020, George Floyd, a forty-six-year-old Black man, was killed in Minneapolis. The protests against his murder that erupted in cities across the United States and throughout the world were a visceral response to the killings of Black Americans by the police.

Between 2014 and 2020, police in the United States killed more than 6,557 people. Twenty-five percent of those killed were Black, despite the fact that Black Americans make up only 13.4 percent of the US population. This is quoted from "Know Their Names — Black People Killed by the Police in the US."[1] and other sources from the news media.

Akai Gurley, 28

Year: 2015 — What she was doing: At home. How she was killed: Four police officers arrived to serve a court-ordered transport to an inpatient mental health facility. Possibly confused, Cusseaux had an exchange with the officer who decided to remove her security door. They said she charged toward them with a hammer. Sergeant Percy Dupra fired a single shot. Cusseaux died shortly after. Action taken: Dupra was demoted.

Alton Sterling

Year: 2016 — What was he doing: Selling CDs and DVDs, Sterling was shot by Officer Blane Salamoni, one of two officers who confronted him outside a shop. He was tasered and pinned to the ground before being shot six times. In video footage, Salamoni can be heard threatening to shoot Sterling in the head and then, after the shooting, repeatedly calling him "a stupid mother fucker." Salmoni was fired. Howie Lake II, the other officer involved, was suspended for three days. No charges were filed.

Anthony Hill, 26

Year: 2015 — How he died: The shooting of Anthony Hill, a US Air Force veteran, occurred in Chamblee, Georgia, near Atlanta. He was fatally shot by US police officer Robert Olsen. Hill suffered from mental illness and was naked and unarmed at the time of the incident. In January 2016, a grand jury indicted Officer Olsen on two counts of felony murder and one count of aggravated assault.

Atatiana Jefferson, 28

Year: 2019 — How she died: A police officer shot and killed Jefferson through the window of her home in the presence of her eight-year-old nephew. The police were responding to a call from a neighbor who reported that Jefferson's front door had been left open. Action taken: Officer Aaron Dean resigned. He was later indicted on murder charges.

Aura Rosser, 40

Year: 2014 — What she was doing: At home. How she was killed: Rosser's boyfriend, Victor Stephens, called 911 to ask the police to escort her out of the house because of an altercation. The official report says that when the officers entered the home, Rosser was holding a knife and refused to drop it. Officer Mark Raab used his taser. Officer David Ried fired a single shot that killed her. Action taken: Ried did not face any charges over Rosser's death. The police department and city implemented reforms, including equipping officers with body cameras.

Botham Jean, 26

Year: 2018 —What was he doing: Seated on his sofa at home, eating ice cream. Jean was shot by off-duty police officer Amber Guyger after she entered his apartment believing, she said, that it was hers and he was a dangerous intruder. Action taken: Guyger was found guilty of murder and sentenced to ten years in prison. The maximum sentence available was ninety-nine years. Prosecutors had asked that she be sentenced to twenty-eight years. Jean's brother, Brandt Jean, hugged Guyger in court and told her he forgave her.

Breonna Taylor, 26

Year: 2020 — What she was doing: Asleep at home. How she was killed: Taylor and her boyfriend, Kenneth Walker, were sleeping when three plainclothes officers arrived at their apartment to execute a search warrant. They believed it was a break-in and Walker called 911 and fired his licensed firearm. Taylor, who was unarmed, was shot eight times. Action taken: Officers involved in the incident were reassigned pending the results of an investigation.

Dante Parker, 36

Year: 2014 — How he died: A person called 911 and identified a man fitting Parker's description who deputies saw riding away from the home on a child-size bicycle, according to the district attorney's report. The deputy who responded tried to arrest Parker, but he became "uncooperative and combative," the sheriff's department said. A physical struggle ensued, during which the deputy stunned Parker with a taser multiple times. Eventually, Parker was handcuffed and placed in the back seat of a patrol unit. Deputies noted that he appeared to be under the influence of an unknown substance. It was then that deputies noticed Parker was sweating profusely and having difficulty breathing, prompting them to call for medical aid, authorities said. Parker was taken by ambulance to the Victor Valley Global Hospital, where he died while receiving treatment, according to the sheriff's department. A federal judge approved a $250,000 global settlement between San Bernardino County and the family of Dante Parker, a deal described as having "made the most sense" by an attorney representing Parker's wife and five children.

Eric Garner,43

Year: 2014 — What he was doing: Allegedly selling loose cigarettes. How he was killed: Officer Daniel Pantaleo held Eric in a chokehold that he did not release in spite of Garner saying "I can't breathe" eleven times. Action taken: A grand jury declined to indict Pantaleo. He was placed on desk duty after the incident. He was fired in 2019. The city reached a settlement with the Garner family for $5.9m.

Ezell Ford, 25

Year 2014: — What was he doing: The officers and eyewitnesses offered competing accounts of the events surrounding the shooting, and an investigation by the LAPD's watchdog unit, Los Angeles Board of Police Commissioners, concluded in June 2015 that one officer had been justified in the shooting, while the other officer was unjustified, had acted outside of LAPD policy, and had violated Ford's civil rights by detaining him. He died from multiple gunshot wounds after being shot by Los Angeles Police Department (LAPD) officers in Florence, Los Angeles, California. A lawsuit by Ford's family claiming $75 million in damages was filed.

After his death, his parents said their son had been diagnosed with depression, bipolar disorder, and schizophrenia, and that everybody in the neighborhood, as well as police, were aware of this. They recalled that Ford had become more introverted and more melancholic around the age of eighteen and took medication that made him less active. The City of Los Angeles settled this lawsuit in October 2016 for $1.5 million.

Frank Smart, 39

Year: 2015 — How he died: Frank Smart, a father of nine, died January 5, 2015, from a seizure after being restrained facedown at the lockup in the Allegheny County Jail. A suit brought by his oldest daughter, Tiara, said that jail personnel did not give him his seizure disorder medication in a timely fashion, which the jail personnel were told he needed when he was brought to the jail. The Allegheny County paid $950K as a settlement to Smart's children as a result of his death from seizures.

Freddie Gray, 25

Year: 2015 — What he was doing: Gray had been arrested and placed in the back of a police van. He was found dead forty-five minutes later, his spinal cord nearly severed. His hands and feet had been shackled and without a seat belt, he could not protect himself as he was tossed around inside the vehicle. Action taken: Six officers were charged in connection with Gray's death. Three were acquitted and three had their cases dropped. The city reached a $6.4m settlement with Gray's family.

Gabriella Nevarez, 22

Year: 2014 — What she was doing: Driving. How she was killed: When officers asked Nevarez to pull over she rammed into a patrol car. The police officers opened fire on her car. Action taken: At least two officers were put on administrative leave.

George Mann, 35

Year: 2015 — How he died: Officers responded to a call on Rock Place Drive after receiving a 911 call that Mann had been acting strangely. In the descriptive two-page narrative, the officer describes Mann yelling from inside of a neighbor's closed garage, shouting "let me out of here" and "I'll shoot all of you." The officer who responded writes that he "attempted to handcuff George" and "gained control of (his) legs to keep him from kicking (the other officer)." "After George was handcuffed, we sat him up and moved him outside to the driveway. When we moved George to the driveway, he stopped flailing and was not responsive." According to the report, officers immediately began performing CPR and used an automated external defibrillator (AED) to try to revive Mann until paramedics arrived. George Mann died while in the custody of Gwinnett County Police.

The case is now under Georgia Bureau of Investigation, but Mann's family is now speaking up because they're concerned they did not get the full story. Mann's family says they were initially told that Mann died of an overdose. But they claim police never told them a Taser was involved, and that they only found out when they saw the report on the news.

Janisha Fonville. 20

Year: 2015 — What she was doing: At home. Officers Anthony Holzhauer and Shon Shefel answered a distress call to take Fonville to a mental health facility. According to Fonville's partner, Korneshia Banks, Fonville had a knife earlier and she was worried she might harm herself. Holzhauer shot Fonville. The official account says Fonville lunged at the officers with knife. Banks says she did not see a knife in Fonville's hand when she was shot. Action taken: Holzhauer was not charged.

Jerame Reid, 36

Year: 2014 — What he was doing: Jerame Reid was killed during a routine two-minute traffic encounter. One of the passengers in the rear seat shouted, "We've got a gun in his glove compartment!" followed by Officer Day saying, "Show me your fucking hands." Days, who appeared to recognize Reid as he was heard calling him by his first name, retrieved a large silver handgun from the glove compartment. Days continued to warn Reid to not move as Reid continued to move his hands around inside the vehicle. Several times, Days exclaimed, "He's reaching for something!" As the situation intensified, someone in the vehicle could be heard telling the officers, "I'm not reaching for nothing. I ain't got no reason to reach for nothing." Reid then told Days, "I'm getting out and getting on the ground." The officer responded, "No, you're not; stay right there, don't move." A struggle ensued as Reid tried to push the door open, and the officer attempted to keep the door closed. Days stepped back, and Reid pushed the door open, got up, and exited the car with his hands at chest level. Days backed up and fired as Reid exited the vehicle. Reid reacted to the shots by moving his hands upwards. Worley fired one shot, and Reid was killed. Reid was unarmed at the time. According to a statement from the Cumberland County Prosecutor's Office, the two officers told investigators that they feared for their lives, believing that Reid was reaching for a weapon. On August 20, 2015, a grand jury voted not to file charges against the two officers involved in the shooting.

John Crawford III, 22

Year: 2014 — How he died: John Crawford, a twenty-two-year-old African American man was shot and killed by a police officer in a Walmart store in Beavercreek, Ohio, while he was holding a BB gun that was for sale in the store. The shooting was captured on surveillance video. Police claimed that Crawford had been pointing the gun at fellow customers. After the security camera footage was released, it showed that "at no point did Crawford shoulder the rifle and point it at somebody." Crawford was talking on his cell phone while holding the BB/pellet air rifle when he was shot to death by Williams. Crawford was later pronounced dead at Dayton's Miami Valley Hospital.

Crawford's mother believes that the surveillance tape shows the police lied in their account of events. A grand jury declined to indict the two officers involved on criminal charges. The City of Beavercreek eventually settled civil claims for $1.7 million for wrongful death brought by Crawford's estate and family.

Joseph Mann, 25

Year: 2014 — What he was doing: Walking down the stairs in the building where he lived. How he was killed: Police officer Peter Liang and his partner were conducting a "vertical patrol" in a housing project. Liang entered an unlit stairwell and fired his weapon. The bullet bounced of a wall and killed Gurley. Action taken: Liang was fired. He was convicted of manslaughter and official misconduct in 2016. He was sentenced to five years' probation and community service.

Laquan McDonald, 17

Year: 2014 — How he died: The murder of Laquan McDonald took place in Chicago, Illinois, when the seventeen-year-old African American was fatally shot by Chicago Police Officer Jason Van Dyke. Police had initially reported that McDonald was behaving erratically while walking down the street and refused to put down a knife he was carrying. Preliminary internal police reports described the incident similarly and ruled the shooting justified and Van Dyke was not charged in the shooting at that time. When a court ordered the police to release a dash cam video of the shooting thirteen months later, on November 24, 2015, it showed McDonald had been walking away from the police when he was shot. That same day, Officer Van Dyke was charged with first-degree murder and initially held without bail at the Cook County Jail. The city reached a settlement with McDonald's family. Van Dyke was found guilty of second-degree murder, as well as sixteen counts of aggravated battery with a firearm. The Chicago City Council approved a $5 million settlement to McDonald's family.

Matthew Ajibade, 22

Year: 2015 — How he died: Ajibade died after being taken into police custody on New Year's Day in the midst of what his family described as a bipolar episode. Graphic video played in court showed how Deputy Jason Kenny used a stun gun on Ajibade while he was in the chair. Officers also placed a spit mask over Ajibade's mouth. He was found dead in the chair, still wearing the spit mask, in the early morning hours of January 2.

Michael Brown. 18

Year: 2014 — What he was doing: Walking with a friend. How he was killed: A white police officer confronted Brown and his friend. A scuffle ensued and the officer — Darren Wilson — shot and killed Brown. Wilson said he acted in self-defense. Action taken: No charges were brought. Wilson resigned from the Ferguson Police Department.

Michael Lee Marshall, 55

Date: 2015 — How he died: Marshall, who was suffering from a psychotic episode, died in November 2015 after he aspirated on vomit while being restrained facedown for more than ten minutes by multiple deputies. The death was a ruled a homicide. City Council approved a $4.65 million settlement that was paid to Marshall's family before a lawsuit was filed.

Michelle Cusseaux, 30

Year: 2015 — What she was doing: At home. How she was killed: Four police officers arrived to serve a court-ordered transport to an inpatient mental health facility. Possibly confused, Cusseaux had an exchange with the officer, who decided to remove her security door. They said she charged toward them with a hammer. Sergeant Percy Dupra fired a single shot. Cusseaux died shortly after. Action taken: Dupra was demoted.

Natasha Mckenna, 37

Year: 2015 — How she died: Natasha McKenna was an African American woman who died while in police custody. While no charges were filed against the deputies who tasered McKenna, the case became the subject of a federal civil rights investigation. She was being held at the Fairfax County Adult Detention Center by the Fairfax County Police Department and Fairfax County Sheriff's Office in Fairfax County, Virginia, due to an outstanding warrant issued over her suspected attack on a police officer. After initially cooperating with officials, there was a weeklong delay in transporting McKenna back to Alexandria, where better assistance could be provided, namely, the resources (i.e., legal representation to petition for a mental health hold) that were required to be provided by the warrant-issuing city. Due to the previous assault charge against her, she was restrained with handcuffs, arms behind her back, her legs shackled, and with a spit mask placed over her head. Seventeen minutes into the forty-five-minute struggle to extract her from her cell, McKenna, who suffered from schizophrenia, was tasered. The specialized team that was called in to address her condition was attempting to ready her for transport to Alexandria, Virginia. The team was made up of six members of the Sheriff's Emergency Response Team (SERT) and was dressed in full-body biohazard suits and gas masks. Shortly after being tasered, McKenna suffered cardiac arrest and lost consciousness, but was resuscitated on the way to Inova Fairfax Hospital by emergency responders. She was placed on life support, but was determined to be brain dead, removed from life support, and pronounced dead on February 8, 2015. The Fairfax County paid a mere $750,000 as a settlement to her family.

Philando Castile, 32

Year: 2016 — How he died: Pulled over for a traffic stop. Police dashcam video of a traffic stop showed a police officer shooting Casile seconds after he informed him that he had a legal firearm. Casile's girlfriend, Diamond Reynolds, who was in the car along with her four-year-old daughter, captured the aftermath on Facebook Live. Jeronimo Yanez was acquitted of second-degree manslaughter.

Stephon Clark, 24

Year: 2018 — What was he doing: He was standing in his grandmother's backyard. The officers said they believed Clark was holding a gun as they shot at him more than twenty times. Clarke was only holding a mobile phone. Action taken: The district attorney declined to file criminal charges. Clark's family reached a $2.4m settlement with the city of Sacramento.

Tanisha Anderson, 37

Year: 2014 — How she was killed: Officers Scott Aldridge and Bryan Myers convinced Anderson to return to a mental health facility. They walked her to their vehicle, but what followed is disputed. The officers said she fell to the ground, while her family said she was slammed down. Investigators estimate that she was handcuffed on the ground for about twenty-one minutes before paramedics arrived. Aldridge was suspended for ten days without pay. Myer was issued a written warning. The city settled a $2.25m wrongful death lawsuit.

Terrill Thomas, 38

Year: 2016 — How he died: He was accused of shooting a man and later firing a gun inside a hotel and casino. A Wisconsin jail commander repeatedly lied after her officers cut off water to Thomas, who later died of dehydration. The commander, Maj. Nancy Evans, was one of three Milwaukee County jail officials charged with a felony in connection with his death.

And finally:

George Floyd

Year: 2020 — How he died: Floyd was handcuffed on the ground as Officer Derek Chauvin knelt on his neck for eight minutes and forty-six seconds — as Floyd pleaded with the four officers present and repeatedly told them that he could not breathe. Chauvin kept his knee on Floyd's neck even when he became unresponsive. Two autopsy reports filed Floyd's death as homicide, although they gave different causes. Action taken: All four officers involved were fired. Chauvin faces the most serious charges, including second-degree murder. The three other officers were charged with aiding and abetting second-degree murder and manslaughter.

———

Others who were killed by police officers between 2014 and 2020 include:

Aaron Bailey, 45

Albert Joseph Davis, 23

Alexia Christian, 26

Alonzo Smith, 27

Alteria Woods, 21

Anthony Ashford, 29

Antronie Scott, 36

Antwon Rose II, 17

Benni Lee Tignor, 56

Bettie Jones, 16

Billy Ray Davis, 39

Brendon Glenn, 29

Brian Keith Day, 59

Calin Roquemore, 23

Christian Taylor, 30

Christopher Davis, 17

Christopher McCorvey, 36

Christopher Whitfield, 31

Darius Robinson, 17

Darrius Stewart, 19

David Joseph, 17

Demarcus Semer, 21

Dominic Hutchinson, 30

Dominique Clayton, 32

Dyzhawn Perkins, 19

Eric Harris, 44

Felix Kumi, 61

India Kager, 27

Jamar Clark, 24

Janet Wilson, 31

Jonathan Sanders, 39

Sandra Bland, 28

Jordan Edwards, 15

Junior Prosper, 31

Keith Childress Jr., 23

Keith Harrison Mcleod,23

Kevin Hicks, 44

Kevin Matthews, 35

La'vante Biggs, 21

Lamontez Jones, 39

Marco Loud, 20

Mary Truxillo, 72

Michael Lorenzo Dean, 28

Michael Noel, 32

Michael Sabbie, 35

Miguel Espinal, 36

Mya Hall, 27

Nathaniel Harris Pickett, 29

Pamela Turner, 44

Paterson Brown, 18

Paul O'Neal, 18

Peter Gaines, 35

Pharoah Manley, 30

Phillip White, 32

Quintonio Legrier, 32

Randy Nelson, 48

Richard Perkins, 39

Ronell Foster, 33

Salvado Ellswood, 36

Samuel Dubose, 43

Sylville Smith, 23

Tamir Rice, 12

Tony Robinson, 19

Torrey Robinson

Troy Robinson Asshams

Tyree Crawford, 22

Victor Manuel Larosa, 23

Walter Scott, 50

Wendell Celestine, 37

William Chapman II, 18

Willie Tillman, 33

APPENDIX 2
AN INVITATION TO BLISSFUL LIVING

These suggestions for blissful living are paraphrased from Candace B. Pert's work *Molecules of Emotions.*[1]

1. Take responsibility for the way you feel.
2. Get enough sleep. If you go to sleep between 10:00 and 11:00 p.m., you'll most likely wake up rested before the break of dawn.
3. Meditate early in the morning and in the evening. Do it routinely.
4. After awakening, fire up your body with gentle stretching or yoga, a brisk walk or run. If you're interested in losing weight, twenty minutes of aerobic exercise early in the morning increases the heart rate and the body enters a smooth, fat-burning mode that lasts for hours.
5. Spend time with nature every day—the mountains, the beach, the open desert . . . at the very least looking at the sky.
6. Don't starve yourself all day and eat a heavy meal at night. Eat your heaviest meal at noon.
7. Restrict the intake of white sugar (sucrose). It turns into glucose which, as it's metabolized, can dramatically affect the way you feel—sluggish, peppy, low, or high. Satisfy the craving for sweets with fruits, which contains a different kind of sugar (fructose).

8. Avoid doing drugs — legal or illegal.

9. Drink two liters of water per day. Sometimes, when you feel hungry, it might be the body's internal signal asking for water.

10. When you're stressed, upset, or feel sick, try to get to the bottom of your emotions, you must attempt to recognize the reason for the suffering and identify the emotions you are experiencing (grief, anger, guilt, embarrassment, fear, confusion, dejection, etcetera).

11. Mindfully work with the situation—recognizing that cessation of the suffering and achieving a state of well-being is possible.

12. Notice the manifestation of well-being — either by resolving the problem, if it's resolvable, or accepting it.

13. Practice and cultivate loving kindness and forgiveness.

APPENDIX 3
OTHER MINDFULNESS INTERVENTIONS

"Do you have the patience to wait
till your mud settles and the water is clear?"

~ Lao Tzu

Although too numerous to describe here in their entirety, the following are other mindfulness exercises the reader may want to look up on the internet.

These are other practices available to you that you may do without any guidance.

- Mindful Seeing Meditation
- Eating or Walking Meditation
- Showering or Bathing Meditation
- Body Scan
- Acceptance of Social Anxiety
- Mountain Meditation
- Lake Meditation
- Breath Focus
- Laughing Yoga
- Five Senses Meditation

Once you integrate mindfulness into the fabric of your daily life, you will find out that anything and everything you do you will be doing mindfully. And instead of *reacting* off the cuff to any unforeseen negative situations, you will be *responding* appropriately. As a result, you will not make others unhappy or make things worse for yourself.

You will be able to accept your selflessness and prepare yourself to confront death with a sense of gratitude and peace. It will help you learn that:

"All Lives Can't Matter Until Black Lives Matter."

AUTHOR'S PAGE

Jaime R. Carlo-Casellas, Ph.D., September 15, 1943 –

My approach and understanding of mindfulness are addressed in great detail in my recently published book, *Mindfulness for the Common Man: to Survive Trauma, Abuse, and Recovery*, as well as in my other two books, *Chaos & Bliss* and *Anguish & Joy*.

My books address the notion that human suffering will always exist as long as superiority persists. We must recognize that we are selfless. Our human experience is without meaning or unworthy of analysis until we mindfully recognize what it means to be happy; until we question why we habitually inflict unhappiness on each other, where the seedbed of loathing, opprobrium, and odium resides.

As you will find in my books, it is now well-known that mindfulness can help you reap a cauldron of benefits, not to mention reach higher brain functioning, achieve loving kindness toward others, as well as help with the management of emotional trauma, abuse, and addictive behavior.

So, my thesis is that as special as we may label ourselves, all our ancestors passed on their DNA not just to create us, but also our many cousins. And, as we can imagine, 130,000 people have a lot of descendants, so it's not surprising that the average "I" can find so many cousins. In our generation, we may well have had hundreds of thousands of ancestors overall, but we still only had one matrilineal ancestor, and that was our "Eve." We all descend from the same maternal womb.[1]

As to my background, I hold a Ph.D. in Experimental Immunopathology, am a Certified Life Coach and Mindfulness Instructor and Consultant, a Registered Yoga Instructor, and have trained in Mindfulness-Based Cognitive Therapy. During the Vietnam Conflict, I served as a Medical Service Corps Officer in the United States Navy. I am also the Founding Director of the Stress Management & Prevention Center, LLC, in Cathedral City, California.

To reach Jaime Carlo-Casellas

email: casellas@stressprevention.org

Phone: 1- (760) 464-2150

AFTERTHOUGHT

Black Scientists Matter

It is well known that racial discrimination occurs in the world of science. As a Hispanic scientist I had often discussed the fact that we are not well-represented or valued in the Western world with other Latino, Black, and foreign scientists. We have often felt as aliens in academia.

The Western world of science is in denial about its inbreed racial discrimination. As splinter group scientists we encounter discrimination as we struggle to embark on scientific careers — to the point that we get frustrated and many of us eventually opt for other careers or simply become independent entrepreneurs.

The overwhelming message, from our experiences, is that the culture of Western science is a world where Hispanic and Black scientists are underrepresented — a world riddled with antipathy beyond dispute. For example, although science is supposed to be objective, behind my back I often heard myself referred to as the "token Puerto Rican" at the institution where I was doing my postdoctoral fellowship.

Some white scientific authorities apodictically believe that the problem is not the system, but how minority group scientists fail to adapt to and cope with the discipline, standards, and work ethics of the science establishment. Such scientists may think that they know what xenophobia is and that they are in a better position to explain it to those who have endured it — how impudent, hypocritical, and insensitive can one be.

Sadly, to paraphrase Professor Makgob, Latino and Black scientists — as well as those from under-represented groups — who do not integrate or abandon their heritage and uniqueness altogether in exchange for the so-called White supremacy attributes, can become academically and socially isolated.

For equal opportunity in the sciences to be addressed and flourish, significant changes have to occur. We must create an environment where all scientists can survive — one that values the human person with dignity, impartiality, social justice, and compassion.

LITERATURE CITED

1. The Heritage Foundation: https://www.heritage.org/.
2. Reyes, R. Hughes, T., and Emmert, M: "Medical examiner and family-commissioned autopsy agree: George Floyd's death was a homicide" *USA TODAY* (McLean) June 1, 2020.
3. Lao, O.; De Gruijter, J. M.; Van Duijn, K.; Navarro, A.; Kayser, M. "Signatures of Positive Selection in Genes Associated with Human Skin Pigmentation as Revealed from Analyses of Single Nucleotide Polymorphisms". Annals of Human Genetics. 2007 May; 71 (3): 354–369.
4. Baker, J.R.: *Race* (Oxford: Oxford University Press. 1974).
5. Heng, H.H.Q.: "The Genome-Centric Concept: Resynthesis of Evolutionary Theory". Bioessays 2009 May;31(5):512-25.
6. Connor, S.: "IQ tests are 'fundamentally flawed' and using them alone to measure intelligence is a 'fallacy,' study finds" *Independent* (London) December 21, 2012.
7. Hall, R.: (1997). "The Psychogenesis of Color Based Racism: Implications of Projection for Dark-Skinned Puertorriqueños". Julian Samora Research Institute, Michigan State University. Archived from the original on January 6, 2011. Retrieved 2012-09-25.
8. Benton, TH: *Theodore Roosevelt*, (New York: Charles Scribner's Sons, 1906), reprinted in Noam Chomsky, "Presidential 'Peacemaking' in Latin America," In These Times, January 5, 2010.
9. Congressional Record, 56th Cong., 1st Sess., April 2, 1900, 3612.
10. Belluck, P. 2019: "Many Genes Influence Homosexuality, Not a Single Gay Gene" *The New York Times* (New York) August 29, 2019.
11. Keiser, J: "Genetics may explain up to 25% of same-sex behavior, giant analysis reveals" (Science Aug. 29, 2019 366:10.1126).
12. The Global Gender Gap Report 2018 (PDF). World Economic Forum. 2018. ISBN 978-2-940631-00-1. Retrieved April 28, 2019.

13. Knorsky, Jerzy: *Conditioned Reflexes and Neuron Organization (1948), and Integrative Activity of the Brain* (Cambridge: Cambridge University Press. 1967).

14. Ibid. 12. Knorsky.

15. Davidson, R.J. and Lutz, A: "Buddha's Brain: Neuroplasticity and Meditation" (Signal Process Mag. January 1, 2008 Jan 1; 25(1): 176–174).

16. Kabat-Zinn, J.: From Wikipedia, the free encyclopedia: https://en.wikipedia.org/wiki/Jon_Kabat-Zinn.

1. Mindfulness in the Western World

1. Razzetti, G.: "What babies and lost wallets can teach us about the never-ending moral debate." Liberationist: https://liberationist.org/is-the-human-nature-good-or-evil/

2. Knaster, Mirka: *Living This Life Fully: Stories and Teachings of Munindra* (Boston: Shambala, 2011).

3. Kabat-Zinn, J. and Borysenko, J.: *Full Catastrophe Living: Using the Wisdom of Your Body & Mind to Face Stress, Pain & Illness* (New York: Bantam Books, 2009).

4. John Parrot: "Blogs About Relaxation, Mindfulness & Meditation": https://www.RelaxLikeaBoss.com (© 2019 John Parrrot).

5. Carlo-Casellas, JR: *Chaos & Bliss: A Journey to Happiness / Caos y Éxtasis: Una Jornada Hacia la Felicidad* (Charleston: Booksurge Publishing, 2008 Pg. 48).

6. Oxford English Dictionary—The Definitive Record of the English Language. https://www.oed.com/ (© 2019 Oxford University Press).

7. Davis, D. and Hayes, J.: "What are the Benefits of Mindfulness" (American Psychological Association July/August 2012, Vol 43, No. 7).

2. Current Administration Encourages White Supremacy and Racial Injustice

1. Broomfield, M.: "Women's March against Donald Trump is the largest day of protests in US history, say political scientists". (London) *Independent*. Archived from the original on January 25, 2017.

2. Wikipedia: The Presidency of Donald Trump. https://en.wikipedia.org/wiki/Presidency_of_Donald_Trump#

3. Lippman, D.: Psychological Disorders and Family Squabbles: 9 Details From the Book by Donald Trump's Niece. Politico, July 7, 2020: https://www.politico.com/news/2020/07/07/nine-details-donald-trump-niece-book-350808

4. Ambardar, S.: "What are the DSM-5 diagnostic criteria for narcissistic personality disorder (NPD)?" Medscape, May 16, 2018.

5. Marano, H.S: "Shrinks Battle Over Diagnosing Donald Trump: Chaos in the White House fuels discord amongst the experts." Psychology Today Jan 31, 2017.

6. Lee, B: *The Dangerous Case of Donald Trump: 27 Psychiatrists and Mental Health Professionals Assess a President* (New York: St. Martin's Press. 2017).

7. Raskin, J: "Do You Need a Psychologist to Tell You Trump is Crazy? Everyday people are perfectly capable of drawing their own conclusions." Psychology Today Jan 22, 2018.

8. "Illegal Withholding" Puerto Rico Hurricane Aid. NBC News: https://www.nbcnews.com/news/latino/house-democrats-slam-trump-admin-illegally-withholding-puerto-rico-hurricane-n1096421.

9. The facts: Hurricane Maria's effect on Puerto Rico Mercy Corps, January 08, 2020: https://www.mercycorps.org/blog/quick-facts-hurricane-maria-puerto-rico.

10. "Tesla solar power arrives in Puerto Rico" BBC News: 25 October 2017: https://www.bbc.com/news/technology-41747065.

11. Cole, D.: "New York Times: Trump considered selling Puerto Rico following Hurricane Maria, former acting Homeland Security chief says" CNN July 12, 2020: https://www.cnn.com/2020/07/12/politics/trump-puerto-rico-hurricane-maria/index.html.

12. From Wikipedia, the free encyclopedia: Trump administration family separation policy. https://en.wikipedia.org/wiki/Trump_administration_family_separation_policy.

13. Levinson, J: "Children separated at border, suffering alarming and prolonged effects: UN rights experts" (UN News 19 October 2018) https://news.un.org/en/story/2018/10/1023712.

14. Moore, R. and Susan, S.: "Inside the Cell Where a Sick 16-Year-Old Boy Died in Border Patrol Care." ProPublica, Dec. 5, 2019: https://www.propublica.org/article/inside-the-cell-where-a-sick-16-year-old-boy-died-in-border-patrol-care

15. Underwood, C.: "Zero-tolerance U.S. immigration policy could have asylum seekers looking at Canada" (CBS News June 19, 2018)

16. Tran, N.T. "How Canadians can help children horrifically detained in U.S. — and Canada" *The Star* (Toronto) June 19, 2018.

17. Jordan, M: 2020 "Judge Urges Release of Migrant Children After 4 Test Positive for Coronavirus in Detention" *The New York Times* (New York) March 29, 2020.

18. Friedman, L. and Plumer, B. 2020: "Trump's Response to Virus Reflects a Long Disregard for Science" *The New York Times* (New York) April 28, 2020.

19. Freking, K. and Lemire, J.: "Trump comeback rally features empty seats, staff infections" ABC News, June 21, 2020: https://abc7news.com/politics/trump-comeback-rally-features-empty-seats-staff-infections/6258530/

20. Sy, S. and Woodruff, J: "Trump's Phoenix speech brings thousands together indoors — in a virus hot spot" PBS NewsHour, Jun 23, 2020: https://www.youtube.com/watch?v=6Or_wbvkhAA

21. Reston, M.: "Trump tries to drag America backward on a very different July 4th" CNN, July 4, 2020: https://www.cnn.com/2020/07/04/politics/donald-trump-mount-rushmore-culture-wars-july-4th/index.html

22. Sukin, G.: "Robert Mueller speaks out on Roger Stone commutation" Axios, July 11, 2020: https://www.axios.com/mueller-stone-prosecuted-convicted-38529378-e6fa-44a6-8465-567c5aa53c1e.html?utm_source=facebook&utm_medium=social&utm_campaign=organic&utm_content=1100

3. Black Lives Matter Movement

1. Hart, G: "Black Lives Matter protests mark historic civil rights movement, UNLV professor says" NBC LAS VEGAS (KSNV) Wednesday, June 10, 2020.

2. Asmelash, L: "Black Lives Matter protests have not led to a spike in coronavirus cases, research says" CNN Wed June 24, 2020: https://www.cnn.com/2020/06/24/us/coronavirus-cases-protests-black-lives-matter-trnd/index.html.

3. Boyle, J: "Defund the police? How about restructuring the police?" *Citizen Times* (Ashville) June 27, 2020.

4. Ortiz, A. and Diaz, J.: "George Floyd Protests Reignite Debate Over Confederate Statues" *The New York Times* (New York) June 3, 2020.

5. Duggan, P.: "The Confederacy Was Built on Slavery. How Can So Many Southern Whites Think Otherwise?". *The Washington Post* (Washington, DC) November 28, 2018.

6. Drucker, P.: Racist RF (June 2, 2020): https://www.druckerreport.-com/post/racist-af.

7. Fung, K.: "Why is it wrong to think my race is superior?" QUORA (June 12, 2015) https://www.quora.com/Why-is-it-wrong-to-think-my-race-is-superior-Sure-Ive-met-lots-of-cool-people-from-other-races-even-been-romantically-involved-but-I-still-feel-a-loyalty-and-kindred-to-my-own-race.

8. Ibid. 4. Baker.

4. Benefits of Mindfulness

1. Carlo-Casellas, J.: *Mindfulness for the Common Man: to Survive Trauma, Abuse, and Recovery* (Palm Springs: Teitlebaum Publishing, 2020) Pg. 25.

2. Carlson LE, Speca M: *Mindfulness-Based Cancer Recovery: A Step-by-Step MBSR Approach to Help You Cope With Treatment and Reclaim Your Life. Oakville*, (Oakland, California: New Harbinger, 2011).

3. Johns, A. Shirley, et al: "Randomized controlled pilot study of mindfulness-based stress reduction for persistently fatigued cancer survivors" (Psycho-Oncology 24:885, 2015).

4. Neff, K.: "Don't Fall into the Self-Esteem Trap: Try a Little Self-Kindness" Mindful February 17, 2016.

5. Kumara, Shakya: "How Mindfulness Boosts Resilience": https://www.brief-mindfulness.com/mindfulness-boosts-resilience/ © 2016 Shakya Kumara.

6. Mak, C., et al.: "Effect of mindfulness yoga programme MiYoga on attention, behaviour, and physical outcomes in cerebral palsy: a randomized controlled trial." (2018) Dev Med Child Neurol. 60:922-932.

7. Black, D.S. and Slavich G.M.: Mindfulness meditation and the immune system: a systematic review of randomized controlled trials.Ann N Y Acad Sci. 2016 Jun; 1373(1): 13–24.

5. But I Don't Have Time to Practice Mindfulness

1. Brach, T.: "Feeling Overwhelmed? Remember "RAIN" Mindful, February 7, 2019.

6. Train the Mind, Change the Brain

1. Goleman, D. and Davidson, R.: *Altered Traits: Science Reveals How Meditation Changes Your Mind, Brain, and Body* (New York: Random House, 2017).
2. Mintie, D. and Staples, J.K.: *Reclaiming Life After Trauma—Reclaiming Life with Cognitive-Behavioral Therapy and Yoga.* (Healing Arts Press, Rochester, 2018).
3. Brewer, J.: *The Craving Mind: From Cigarettes to Love—Why We Get Hooked and How We can Break Bad Habits* (Yale University Press: New Haven, 2017).
4. Bowen, S., Witkiewitz, K., Clifasef, S, et al.: "Relative Efficacy of Mindfulness-Based Relapse Prevention, Standard Relapse Prevention, and Treatment as Usual for Substance Use Disorders - A Randomized Clinical Trial" JAMA Psychiatry. 2014;71(5):547-556.
5. Ibid. 62. Goleman and Davidson.
6. Bergland, C.: "Mindfulness and the Vagus Nerve Share Many Powers" (Psych.Today, Feb 5, 2016).
7. Porges, S.W.: *The Polyvagal Theory: Neurophysiological Foundations of Emotions, Attachment, Communication, and Self-regulation* (NewYor: W. W. Norton & Company) 2011.
8. Ibid. 68. Porges Location 1300 (Kindle Edition).
9. Ibid. 68. Porges Location 1300 (Kindle Edition).
10. Hanson, Rick. Buddha's Brain: The Practical Neuroscience of Happiness, Love, and Wisdom New Harbinger, California, 2009) Kindle Edition.
11. Carlson, L.E., Speca, M., Patel, K.D. et al., "Mindfulness-based stress reduction in relation to quality of life, mood, symptoms of stress and levels of cortisol, dehydroepiandrosterone sulfate (DHEAS) and melatonin in breast and prostate cancer outpatients" (Psychoneuroendocrinology, 2004: 29(4):448–74).
12. EOC Institute: The "Calm Chemical" — How Meditation Boosts GABA https://eocinstitute.org/meditation/meditation-boosts-your-gaba/ (© 2019 EOC Institute, San Francisco).
13. Ibid. 62. Goleman and Davidson Pg. 158.
14. Ibid. 62. Goleman and Davidson Pg. 217.
15. Nataraja, Shanida: Revised and Updated: *The Blissful Brain: Neuroscience and Proof of the Power of Meditation.* Kindle Edition. (© 2014 Shanida Nataraja).

16. Ibid. 62. Goleman and Davidson Pg. 232.
17. van der Kolk, Bessel: *The Body Keeps the Score: Brain, Mind, and Body in the Healing of Trauma*, (New York: Penguin Books, 2014).
18. Ibid. 21. Carlo-Casellas Pg. 36.

7. Mindfulness of the Breath

1. Satchidananda, S.S.: *The Yoga Sutras of Patanjali* (Buckingham: Integral Yoga Publications, 1990).
2. Segal, Z., Williams, J., Teasdale, J. *Mindfulness-Based Cognitive Therapy for Depression; A New Approach to Preventing Relapse* (New York: Guilford, 2002).
3. Brown, R., and Gerbarg., P.: *The Healing Power of the Breath: Simple Techniques to Reduce Stress and Anxiety, Enhance Concentration, and Balance Your Emotions* (Boston; Shambala, 2012).
4. Gordon, J: *The Transformation Discovering Wholeness and Healing After Trauma* (New York: Harper Collins, 2019).

8. Mindfulness on our Domains of Being

1. Seymour, D.: *Psychology Home Study Course By Dr. Dolores Seymour* (Self-Published on Amazon, 2014): https://www.amazon.com/Psychology-Study-Course-Dolores-Seymour/dp/B00L5NX0OE.
2. Ibid. 21. Carlo-Casellas Page 122.
3. Carlo-Casellas, J.R.: *Anguish & Joy / Amargura y Deleite* (Palm Springs: Teitlebaum & Bertrand Publishing, 2018).

9. The Science of Western Yoga

1. Swami Vivekananda: *Raja Yoga & Patanjali Yoga Sutra* (Kindle Edition) https://www.goodreads.com/book/show/18940322-raja-yoga-patanjali-yoga-sutra-by-swami-vivekananda.
2. Kraftsow, G.: "The Yoga of Relationship with Author and Founder of American Viniyoga Institute Gary Kraftsow" Yoga Alliance Webinar, July 2, 2020.

3. Sadhguru: "What is Tantra Yoga? Definitely Orgasmic, But Not Sexual" Isha, June 15, 2020: https://isha.sadhguru.org/us/en/wisdom/article/about-tantra-yoga.
4. Frawley, A.D.: "Vedic Light and Tantric Energy Yogas" American Institute of Vedic Studies: https://www.vedanet.com/vedic-light-and-tantric-energy-yogas-2/.
5. Emerson, D. and West, J: *Trauma-Sensitive Yoga in Therapy: Bringing the Body into Treatment* (New York: W.W. Norton & Co. New York, 2015).
6. Ibid. 78. van der Kolk Pg. 71.
7. Miller, Richard: "Transforming Negative Thoughts with Meditation" Yoga Journal Nov. 14, 2016.
8. The HeartMath Inner Balance app is an innovative approach to improving wellness through training, education, and self-monitoring. Inner Balance helps get your heart, mind, and emotions in sync (coherence) to improve health, well-being, and performance. https://apps.apple.com/us/app/inner-balance/id569278747.
9. Ibid. 84. "The Golden Castle" Audio Recording
10. *Candlelight Impressions* (A self-published book) (Author unnamed for confidentiality).

10. Loving Kindness

1. Hanh, T.N. "The Four Qualities of Love" (Creative by Nature): https://creativesystemsthinking.wordpress.com/2015/02/15/the-four-qualities-of-love-by-thich-nhat-hanh/.
2. Kabat-Zinn, J: "This Loving Kindness Meditation is a Radical Act of Love: Jon Kabat-Zinn leads us in a heartscape meditation for deep healing of ourselves and others." Mindful, November 8, 2018.
3. Ibid. 98. Kabat-Zinn.
4. Ibid. 86. Carlo-Casellas Pg. 180.

11. Autogenics

1. Brunner J, Schrempf M, Steger F. Johannes Heinrich Schultz and National Socialism. Isr J Psychiatry Relat Sci. 2008;45(4):257-62.

2. Cuncic, A.: "Autogenic Training for Reducing Anxiety" VerywellMind, November 29, 2019: https://www.verywellmind.com/how-to-practice-autogenic-training-for-relaxation-3024387#citation-2

12. Walking Meditation

1. Ibid. 21. Carlo-Casellas Pg. 112.
2. Bertin, M.: "A Daily Mindful Walking Practice" Mindful July 17, 2017: https://www.mindful.org/daily-mindful-walking-practice/

13. Body Awareness

1. Kabat-Zinn, J.: *Coming to Our Senses* New (York: Hyperion Press, 2005).
2. Ibid. 83. Gordon Pg. 174.
3. Netter, F.H.: *Atlas of Human Anatomy* (Philadelphia; Elsevier, 2019)

14. Sitting Meditation

1. Ibid. 84. Carlo-Casellas Pg. 246.

15. Shaking and Swaying

1. Ibid. 83. Gordon Pg. 66.
2. Ibid. Carlo-Casellas Pg. 40

Appendix 1 - The Protests

1. "Know Their Names — Black People Killed by the Police in the US": https://interactive.aljazeera.com/aje/2020/know-their-names/index.html

Appendix 2 - An Invitation to Blissful Living

1. Pert, C.B.: *Molecules of Emotions — The Science Behind Mind-Body Medicine.* (New York: Scribner, 1997).

Author's Page

1. Bryc, K.: "Everyone Is Related. The (Big) Data Proves It" X23andMeBlog, March 23, 2015, under Ancestry Reports: https://blog.23andme.com/ancestry-reports/everyone-is-related-the-big-data-proves-it/#:~:text= (host%20of%20%E2%80%9CFinding%20Your%20-Roots,two%2C%20or%20three%20DNA%20cousins.